Agathos
The Rocky Island
and Other Stories

Agathos
The Rocky Island
and Other Stories

Chris Wright

Lighthouse Publishing

Agathos
The Rocky Island
and Other Stories

Copyright ©2007 Chris Wright

Scripture quotations are taken from:
New American Standard Bible (NASB) Copyright © 1960, 1962, 1963, 1968, 1971, 1972, 1973, 1975, 1977, 1995 by The Lockman Foundation

All rights reserved. Without limiting the rights under copyright reserved above, no part of this publication may be reproduced, stored in a retrieval system, or transmitted, in any form or by any means (electronic, mechanical, photocopying, recording or otherwise), without the prior written permission of the copyright owner of this book.

Published by
Lighthouse Christian Publishing
SAN 257-4330
5531 Dufferin Drive
Savage, Minnesota, 55378
United States of America

www.lighthouseebooks.com
www.lighthousechristianpublishing.com

CONTENTS

INTRODUCTION	2
THE KING AND HIS SERVANTS	5
A LESSON OF FAITH	23
THE ROCKY ISLAND	31
WAITING	42
THE WANDERERS	50
NOT LOST, BUT GONE BEFORE	60
AGATHOS	77
COBWEBS	86
THE SPRING MORNING	96
EPILOGUES	117
THE WRITERS	135

Agathos, The Rocky Island and Other Stories

INTRODUCTION

Allegories are stories with a hidden meaning, and this is a book of allegories. I first revised a selection of these classic stories for young readers in 1980. I have enjoyed going through every story again to produce this brand new book. I have also added two further stories.

So what exactly have I done to the originals? Think of a writer adapting a book for a film or a television program. The writer takes a story and reshapes it to make it more suitable for the chosen audience. So too here, I have taken nine stories by two great writers. I make no claims to have invented them – only adapted them for this book so today's readers can gain more from them.

Samuel Wilberforce and Margaret Gatty wrote their stories over a hundred and fifty years ago. I have many happy memories of my father reading these allegories to me when I was young, from old books that I still have today. He updated the language as he went along and often simplified and explained incidents, exactly as I have done here – but he was able to do it while he read! I loved the pictures in these books, and I have reproduced many of them here, although a few come from natural history books of the same period.

There is something special about the way these stories were first written, and I have tried to preserve this old-fashioned feeling. Some of these allegories are about kings, a dangerous forest – and a knight called Agathos who fights a dragon. There are also stories about spiders, caterpillars and dragonflies. And of course there's a rocky island! This is a book with a mix of stories that will appeal to all ages, including parents.

It is easy to pick holes in Christian allegories like these, and say that the Christian life isn't exactly like this or like that. Of course it's not. Stories like these are meant to get us thinking, and make us face up to where we are in life. So please don't get hung up about the details and wonder what everything stands for – you need to look at the big picture.

Many readers will quickly spot the hidden meanings in these stories, but here is a bit of help: musical instruments are prayer, and a compass is the Bible. For anyone who wants to think a little more deeply about the allegories, there is a short epilogue for each story starting on page 117. Some of the Bible verses in the epilogues are clearly what the original writers had in mind.

I am not using capitals for *king* and *prince*, or for words like *son*, *he*, *me* and so on when they refer to the king and the prince, because the story characters are *not* God the Father and Jesus the Son, although they are very much like them – which, of course, is the whole point of these allegories.

This book is not for someone who wants to read the originals exactly as they were written, but for readers who would never consider reading "old-fashioned books." However, copies of the original Victorian volumes can often be bought on internet sites like www.abebooks.com and modern reprints are sometimes available from sellers such as Amazon. It is also worth searching to see if copies can be downloaded free from sites like Project Gutenberg. Nevertheless, in their original form these stories would be hard going for all but the most determined young readers – and probably for many older ones.

Chris Wright
Bristol
England

THE KING AND HIS SERVANTS
Samuel Wilberforce

A great king once called his servants to him. "You have often claimed you love me and wish to serve me," he told them. "Well, the time has come to find out if you really mean what you say. I want you all to prepare for a long journey, and be ready to leave early tomorrow morning."

With this, the king dismissed his servants and they began to talk to each other in great excitement. A long journey? What sort of test would it be? That night many of them stayed up late, getting ready. They told their friends that even if the test was a difficult one they wanted to show the king just how much they cared for him. Others sat quietly, wondering if they would be good enough to do well in whatever test the king was planning.

Now, all these servants had once been held prisoner in a dark dungeon by a cruel and wicked enemy, who had made them work for him. But all that was in the past, for the king had sent his son the prince to rescue them, promising crowns and much more to every servant who served him faithfully.

However, not all the servants were brave, but the ones who felt most anxious remembered how kind and loving the king and his son had been. So even though they were afraid they might fail, these servants joined with the bolder, less fearful ones as they made ready.

As soon as the sun rose the next day, the servants went to the palace court where the king greeted them as they waited to hear what the test was to be.

"I have opened my treasure house," the king said. "I have brought out gold and silver and other precious things. I am giving them to you as gifts. Far away from my palace, across the desert, is a great city. In that city there are many merchants. I want you to take these gifts and trade them in the marketplace, but you must use them wisely. When the time comes for you to return I want you to bring back many wonderful things."

The servants felt overjoyed when they heard this, and went forward to receive the treasures the king had to offer. Trading for their king? Surely this must be the most exciting test ever.

The king saw the excitement on his servants' faces, but he held his hand up in warning. "In that city," he said solemnly, "there are people who will try to rob you of your gifts. Be on your guard every minute of the day, and do not waste your time. Remember, you will be coming back to show me what you have done."

When they heard this, the servants held onto their treasures tightly. No one was going to steal from them or make them waste *these* precious gifts.

The king explained to his servants that the morning was the best time for trading in the market of that city, when all the finest goods would be on sale. He warned them that unless they were early, many of the best things would be gone.

"At the end of the day," he said, "you will hear the sound of a trumpet. That trumpet call is to summon you home. Make sure you do not return to me empty-handed."

Several of the servants looked at each other in alarm. To hear the trumpet call and to have wasted their time would be a disgrace indeed. To come back with nothing to offer the king was unthinkable. They finished packing their bags slowly and thoughtfully.

They knew that their journey across the vast desert would be long and hard, and no sand must get into their precious bundles to harm the goods. However, not all the servants packed carefully enough to be sure that all their gifts would be easy to find when they arrived at the great city. Indeed, only a few seemed to remember the king telling them to begin their trade in the early morning.

Some servants laughed at the careful ones. "There will be

time enough to sort our gifts out when we get there," they said. But when the journey was over, and they arrived at the city gates and pitched their tents, these same servants decided to leave their unpacking until the next morning.

"The journey has been long and hot and difficult," these lazy servants complained. "We need to rest and find plenty to eat and drink."

So they went off to enjoy themselves, forgetting the king's advice.

As the sun rose the next morning, many of the servants jumped up quickly and began to get ready. They talked excitedly of what lay before them inside in the city as they traded for their king. The servants who had stayed up late turned in their sleep and told everyone to be quiet. But the ones who had been careful to do exactly as the king told them, took no notice and hurried through the city gates with their goods on their backs.

What a great city it was. They could see streets and houses going in all directions. Most of the inhabitants seemed to be still asleep, so the king's servants were able to walk quickly and easily in spite of the large packs on their backs. When they reached the marketplace they began to display their precious wares.

The merchants from the city gathered round to see what they had to offer. Then in return they showed the servants what treasures they had.

It was exactly as the king had said. The merchants gave the servants first choice of all their wares. There were rubies and diamonds, and pearls such as the servants had never seen before for size and beauty. A merchant showed one servant a large, flawless pearl that was so valuable it was called the pearl of great price. The servant traded all he had come with to buy it for his king, while others continued to trade wisely until they had more and better treasures than they had brought with them.

A few of the servants were more skillful than their companions at trading, but each made the best use he could of his abilities. Apart from precious jewels and pearls, some bought beautiful robes adorned with gold and silver. Still others acquired spices from afar, and precious perfume from the islands of the East.

One servant seemed to have nothing to carry home. His friends asked him what he had done with his gifts.

The King and His Servants

"I have no riches to show you," the servant told them. "But in my pack I have an offering that I know the king will treasure, because of his mercy and kindness."

The other servants gathered round and begged him to tell his story.

"I was walking through the market," the servant said, "when I saw a poor woman standing all alone and crying to herself. I asked her why she was so sad. I thought her heart would break as she told me how her husband had borrowed a large sum of money from some men, and now he was dead. She said the men had come round in the night to demand their money, but it had been spent long ago. So the men forced their way into her house and took everything she had. Worse than that, they were about to sell her children as slaves so they could get their money back in full."

The other servants listened, grim faced at the thought of such heartless men.

"You will not wonder that I opened my pack of treasure and offered to repay the debt," the servant explained. "There was only just sufficient to pay back the money the widow owed and set her children free. But now the family can live in peace."

The servant held up a small glass container like a perfume bottle, filled with a clear liquid. "I have no treasure of precious stones to take back to our king," he said. "All I have are the woman's tears and thankfulness, but I believe the king will be pleased with what I bring."

The other servants told him that this was surely one of the best gifts with which any of them could return. They continued trading as they thought about how much the king must love them, remembering the time they had been prisoners in the enemy's dungeon, and how the prince had come to rescue them. Their hearts filled with thanks, and they were glad to be taking precious merchandise back to their king.

How excited they said they would be when the trumpet sounded. They did not know when that would be, but whenever it sounded loud and clear, they would be going in gladness to meet their king.

The sun was now high in the sky and the city was becoming busy, all very different from the time when the streets were nearly deserted. People poured out of their houses – some for work, others to enjoy themselves, and still others to do nothing but watch the crowds passing by. The servants were indeed glad they had set about their trading early.

The merchants were already closing their richest stores, and men with imitation pearls and fake jewelry were taking their place. There appeared to be hardly any honest traders left in the marketplace. Noisy people pushed their way through the crowds, and men called out to announce traveling sideshows. In the shadows, at the edge of the marketplace, the servants noticed a gang of men lying in wait to see whom they could catch and rob.

The king's servants held their treasures even more tightly. Of course, some of the things they saw were good to look at, and some of the music was indeed pleasant. Bands of musicians and singers walked up and down through the market. The servants enjoyed the good things in the city, but always remembered their king and his son. Even when the lights were at their brightest, and the music was at its most appealing, these servants were always ready for the trumpet that would call them home. Not one of them wanted to be ashamed of what he was doing when the call came to return.

If only this was so with all the king's servants. When the first servants set out early, those who had stayed up late remained in their tents and complained about the noise. True, some nearly got up to join the early risers, but they had not yet prepared their goods for trading. So they decided they might as well wait until everyone else was ready, and then go to the market together. They certainly did not intend to be late, but saw no reason why they should be so early.

They slept until the sun was high, and rose in a rush when they realized how late it was. All their goods had to be unpacked and sorted, and the dust of the journey had to be shaken off. These servants were secretly angry with themselves, but they blamed each other, and everyone argued fiercely. So instead of making the best use of what time remained, they made themselves even later.

In the end, after many harsh words and much bad temper, they finally got going. Some still had their goods in a muddle, but off they went, each making his own way to the market instead of helping each other find the safest route.

As soon as they entered the city gates, these lazy servants found everyone pushing and pulling this way and that. People laughed at the way they were dressed, and when they at last opened their packs in the market to begin trading, children gathered round and made fun. There seemed to be no way these servants could trade their precious gifts.

Some, who had boasted loudly that they hoped the test would be a hard one, were the first to admit defeat when the crowd made things difficult. So they packed up their goods and joined with the throng until it was difficult to tell them apart. On and on the remaining servants pushed, to a place where there was a large show tent. A man stood outside blowing a trumpet, while another shouted an invitation to everyone to come and see the strange sights within.

One of the servants stood watching as the people of the city crowded into the huge tent. Then he too went to the entrance. The showman asked for his money, but when he saw that the coins belonged to another country, he turned the servant away.

"Stand back!" he commanded.

As the servant walked away, the showman saw the pack of precious gifts and immediately changed his tone. "My friend, do not go," he called. "Give me your pack of goods and I will let you in."

For a moment the servant stopped. He thought of the king, and how he had told all the servants to use their gifts wisely. He almost made up his mind to make his way back to the marketplace and trade for the king, cost him what it might, but at that moment a burst of sound came from the showman's trumpet, and he heard the shouts of excitement from inside the tent. Quickly he forgot the king's instructions, and as fast as he could slip the pack from his shoulders and hand it to the showman, the servant was inside.

Another of the king's servants stood at the corner of a street watching some jugglers. He was so captivated that he forgot all about trading for his master, and thought of nothing but the performers. As he watched so intently, some men crept up behind him and without his knowing they stole the gold from his pack. The servant continued to stare at the show. When he came to trade he would discover his loss, and when the trumpet sounded he would have nothing to take back for the king.

Other servants were treated even more badly. One of them followed the excited crowds from street to street until he came to the very edge of the city. Across some fields he fancied he saw even more exciting sights. No sooner did he set out, than the gang of men rushed from their hiding place and beat him up. With his goods gone, he hardly had the strength to get back to the city.

Another of these lazy servants became frightened as he watched the people entering the showman's tent. One of his friends asked him why he trembled. At first he could not answer, but after a while he explained that he had just heard the showman's trumpet, and it reminded him of his master's great trumpet sound that was yet to come. He had been frightened because much of the day had gone already, and he had not even begun to trade for the king.

"How can we stand before our king with our hands empty?" he asked his friends.

His companions jeered, but this servant knew his fears were wiser than their laughter. "You are in the same danger," he told them. "How then can you make fun of me?" He pointed at the sky and showed them how low the sun was getting. "The trumpet may sound at any moment, and we will have nothing to take back."

As this servant spoke, one of his friends listened in shame. "What can we do?" he asked. "Have we left it too late?"

"It is never too late – until the trumpet sounds," the servant said. "Even though we have wasted much of the day, there must be *something* we can do. Come with me to the marketplace and we will see."

The second servant agreed. Off they set, pushing their way past old friends who shouted and laughed at them. This disturbance made the people of the city join in. The two servants looked at each other and wished once more that they had set out early to the market to trade their gifts. The people in the crowd were rude to them, and at times angry.

"Pushing through this crowd is like swimming against a swift river," said the servant who had been persuaded to come by his friend. "Do you think we will ever get there?"

"Yes, yes," his companion cried. "We will get there if we keep going."

The other was not so sure. "It is so *hard*. The streets seem to get more and more full. I feel very afraid."

Just as he spoke, a huge group of the townspeople met them like a mighty wave of the sea. There was music and trumpets and dancing, and all this seemed sure to drive the two servants back. They could even see one of their old friends dancing among the rest. He was the man who had given away his pack of treasures to go into the showman's tent. As soon as he saw the two servants, he called to them by their names and invited them to join with the crowd.

The servant who was leading the way shook his head. "No, we're going to the marketplace to trade for our king."

The man mocked him. "It's too late for that. You should have gone there in the morning. There's no point in going *now!*"

The first servant who had been so afraid earlier, turned pale, but still kept on his way. "You are right," he called. "We wasted the morning and much of the afternoon, and it makes me sad. But our good king will help us even now, and we *will* serve him."

Then the servant who was with the crowd turned to the servant's companion. "Your friend has gone mad. What's the use of going to the market when it's closed? Come on, join in our fun."

The second servant hung his head in shame. He would have joined with the crowd, if his friend had not seized him by the hand and told him not to listen.

With that, the second servant seemed to get stronger, and he held tightly to his friend as they pushed on.

Their former companion turned on them in hate. He shouted to the people to grab hold of the two and stop them. The noisy crowd would have done this if the two servants had not managed to push their way through, using a strength that seemed to come from beyond. Almost immediately they found themselves in another street.

There were fewer people here, and the two servants paused to recover their breath. But as they, they could hear the crowd and its music in the distance.

"I could never have held on without your help," the second servant said.

"You must not thank me," his companion replied. "It was our king who gave us the strength."

"Then do you think he will accept what we can get, even

though the day is nearly over? Oh, my friend, I wish I had your courage. I am so afraid that if I meet that crowd again they will tear us to pieces."

"Our king will never let that be," his friend said. "We must trust him."

Just then the crowd of singers, dancers and musicians came bursting round the corner. Leading them was their former companion who had urged them to join the crowd. When he saw this, the servant who had been so frightened before became even more anxious now.

Close by, the two servants could see a large shop. In the window shone what appeared to be precious stones, many of them set in metal the color of gold. The second servant turned quickly to his friend.

"Look," he said. "Surely here is all we need. Let us go in and trade for our lord and master. We will also escape from the crowd."

"No, no!" his friend cried. "We must make our way to the marketplace, for that is where the king told us to trade. Being late has brought us troubles, but this shop has nothing good enough to take back for our master. Stay close and we will soon be there."

The second servant held back. "Look, the crowd is coming over. See how many people there are!" He turned to the shopkeeper.

"Come in, come in," the shopkeeper said, hurrying outside to greet him. "Hurry, before the crowd sweeps you away. Come in and buy my beautiful jewels. My rubies, my garnets, my emeralds. Rare jewels. Come in, come in."

While the second servant paused to hear what the shopkeeper had to offer, the crowd pushed past and the two servants became separated. The second servant realized his friend had gone, and without further thought he hurried into the shop hoping to be safe.

The shopkeeper seemed to be an honest man, but his gleaming goods were worthless. If it had been earlier, the clear morning light would have shown the imitation jewelry for what it was. The brightness of the day was fading now, and the glow of the evening sun made the deception hard to detect.

So the shopkeeper persuaded the servant to part with his riches, and gave him nothing in return but bits of colored glass. What a poor showing these would make when presented to the king.

The servant had no idea he had been cheated. Or if the thought crossed his mind that something might be wrong, he knew he must now take the blame for wasting his time and his gifts. As he left the shop the servant stared down the road wishing he had stayed with his companion.

And what a hard struggle his companion faced before he finally got to the market. At times it seemed as if the words of his former friend were coming true, and he really would be torn to pieces as the crowd pressed fiercely against him from all directions.

Suddenly the angry crowd parted like a stream around a rock, and he went through without the people even noticing him. At last he reached the marketplace. How glad he was to find himself there, but even so his troubles were not over. Many of the stalls were empty, and at others there were only dealers in imitation jewelry and poor quality goods.

The servant looked around anxiously, afraid that the trumpet would sound before he had a chance to purchase anything for his king. Now he was more than sorry that he had wasted so much of the day. "What shall I do?" he said to himself. "How can I trade for my master when I've wasted my time so badly?"

Then he noticed a stall where there were no jewels, no gold or costly silk, no pearl of great price. All he could see were rough garments and coarse sackcloth, and behind these were ashes and loaves of sour bread. Some bottles containing tears rested on leaves of bitter herbs. As the servant gazed at the stall, something seemed to whisper to him, "Go and buy."

The servant knew deep inside that he was not good enough to trade for his master, but full of sorrow he stepped forward and with trembling hands bought the roughest sackcloth, the ashes and the saddest tears. It was his way of saying to the king that he was truly sorry. After trading his gifts for these, the servant stepped back into the marketplace to wait for the trumpet.

Then suddenly through the evening air came its clear voice, growing louder and louder. The sound pealed across the sky, and the great city with its shows and its noise and its excitement melted away to nothing. Immediately the servants found themselves gathered together, standing with their king. Everything had gone, except the servants and their belongings.

The king called them forward so he could see what they had brought. The servants who had risen early and traded their gifts wisely were given crowns of light and much gladness. Each servant had his own reward. The man who had the poor widow's tears and grateful thanks seemed to bring a gift that pleased the king more than many others.

Then the servant who had wasted the day but had bought the sackcloth and ashes and tears stepped forward slowly, and his offering was indeed poor to look at. The king placed it amongst the heaps of gold and jewels and precious cloth. The servant looked up at the king and said, almost silently, "I have read that you do not wish anyone to perish, but for all to come to repentance. I am truly sorry."

And as he spoke, the king looked gently at his servant and smiled. "You are a good and faithful servant."

As the king said this, the coarse sackcloth suddenly shone like cloth woven from threads of gold. The ashes sparkled like the finest jewels, and the tears of sadness turned to pearls more valuable than any the king already possessed.

Finally, the king turned to his careless servants, and as he spoke they ran to hide. The king ordered them away from his presence, away from the palace where there was peace and life. The servants who had loved the king, and traded their gifts wisely in the great city, were invited to live in the wonderful light of the palace, while those who had wasted everything were shut outside.

Epilogue on page 117

A LESSON OF FAITH
Margaret Gatty

"Let me hire you as a nurse for my poor children," a butterfly said to a large green caterpillar who was strolling along the leaf of a large cabbage in her odd, lumbering way.

"See these little eggs?" the butterfly continued in a sad voice. "I do not know how long it will be before they come to life, and I feel very sick and poorly. If I should die, who will take care of my tiny butterflies when I am gone? Will you help them, kind caterpillar? You must be careful what you give them to eat. They cannot, of course, live on your rough food."

The poor butterfly wiped her eyes and continued to give the puzzled caterpillar her instructions. "You must give them early dew, and honey from flowers. And you must let them fly, but only a little way at first – for, of course, one cannot expect them to use their wings properly all at once. Dear me, what a pity it is that you cannot fly yourself. But I have no time to look for another nurse now, so please do your best."

A Lesson of Faith

The caterpillar stared at the butterfly in dismay, wondering how she could possibly care for baby butterflies.

The butterfly shook her head. "Dear, dear, I cannot think what made me come and lay my eggs on a cabbage leaf. What a place for young butterflies to be born. And to think how many beautiful plants and blossoms I have visited this glorious summer. Still, you will be kind to my poor little ones, won't you? Take this glittering dust from my wings as a reward. Oh, how dizzy I am. You will remember about the food."

With these words the butterfly drooped her wings and died. The caterpillar, who had not been given the chance to say yes or no to the request, was left standing alone by the side of the butterfly's eggs.

"A pretty nurse she's chosen indeed, poor lady," the caterpillar exclaimed. "And a pretty business I have in hand. Why, that butterfly's senses must have left her, or she never would have asked a poor, crawling creature like me to bring up her dainty little ones. Much notice they'll take of me, truly, when they discover the wings on their backs, and fly away out of my sight whenever they choose. Ah, how silly some people are, in spite of their painted clothes and the beautiful dust on their wings."

However, the poor butterfly was dead, and there lay the eggs on the cabbage leaf. The green caterpillar had a kind heart, so she resolved to do her best. But she got no sleep that night, for she felt extremely anxious. She made her back ache from walking around the eggs, for fear any harm should come to them. In the morning she said to herself, "Two heads are better than one. I shall consult some wise animal on the matter and get advice."

But still there was a difficulty – whom should she consult? There was the shaggy dog who sometimes came into the garden. But he was so rough. If she called him, he would most likely whisk the eggs off the cabbage with one brush of his tail, and then she would never forgive herself. There was the cat, to be sure, who sometimes sat at the foot of the apple tree warming his fur in the sunshine. But he was selfish, so there was no hope of his troubling himself to think about *butterfly* eggs.

"I wonder which is the wisest of all the animals I know," the caterpillar sighed in great distress. And she thought and thought, until at last she remembered the lark. Because he went from place to place and was very inquisitive, surely he must be extremely clever and know a great deal. To fly through the air – which she could never do – was the caterpillar's idea of perfect glory.

Now, in the neighboring cornfield there lived a lark, and the caterpillar sent a message begging him to come and talk

A Lesson of Faith

to her. When the lark came she told him her problem, and asked him how to feed and rear the little creatures so different from herself.

"Perhaps you will be able to inquire and hear something about it next time you fly away," the caterpillar suggested timidly.

The lark said perhaps he might, and went singing away into the bright blue sky. His voice died away in the distance until the caterpillar could no longer hear a sound. Even when she reared herself up most carefully, which she did now, she could neither see nor hear the lark.

She dropped on her legs again, and resumed her walk around the eggs, nibbling at the cabbage leaf now and then as she moved along.

"What a long time the lark has been gone," she cried at last. "I wonder where he is now. How I'd like to know what he hears in that curious, blue sky."

Then the caterpillar took another turn around the butterfly eggs.

At last she heard the lark's voice again. She almost jumped for joy, and it was not long before she saw him descend to the ground beside the cabbages.

"News, news, glorious news, friend caterpillar," the lark sang. "But the worst of it is, you won't believe me."

"I believe everything I'm told," the caterpillar observed hastily.

"Well, then, first of all, I'll tell you what these little creatures need to eat." The lark nodded his beak towards the eggs. "What do you think it is? Guess."

"Early morning dew, and the honey out of flowers, I'm afraid," the caterpillar sighed.

"No such thing, young lady. Something simpler than that. Something you can get easily."

"I can get nothing easily – except cabbage leaves," the caterpillar murmured in distress.

"Excellent, my good friend," the lark cried. "You have found it out. You are to feed them with the leaves of cabbages."

"*Never!*" the caterpillar replied indignantly. "It was their dying mother's last wish that I should do no such thing."

"Their dying mother knew nothing about the matter," the lark persisted. "But why do you ask me, and then disbelieve what I say? You have neither faith nor trust."

"Oh, I believe everything I'm told," the caterpillar insisted.

"No, you don't," the lark replied. "You won't believe me about the food, and yet that's only the beginning of what I have to tell you. Why, caterpillar, what do you think those little eggs will turn out to be?"

"Butterflies, of course," the caterpillar said.

"*Caterpillars!*" chirped the lark. "And you will find it out in time." Then he flew away, for he did not want to stay and

A Lesson of Faith

argue.

"I thought the lark would be wise and kind," the caterpillar complained loudly, once more beginning to walk in circles around the eggs. "But now I know he's foolish and insulting instead. Perhaps he flew too high this time. Ah, it's a pity when people who fly so high are silly and rude. But I still wonder whom he sees, and what he does up yonder."

"I would tell you, if you would only believe me," the lark sang, descending once more.

"I believe everything I'm told," the caterpillar repeated, with as solemn a face as if it were a fact.

"Then I'll tell you something else," the lark cried, "for the best news remains. One day, you will be a butterfly yourself."

"Wretched bird!" the caterpillar exclaimed. "You are making fun of me, so now you're cruel as well as foolish. Go away. I will ask your advice no more."

"I said you would not believe me," the lark said angrily.

"I believe everything I'm told," the caterpillar persisted. "That is . . ." and she hesitated, "everything it is *reasonable* to believe. But please don't tell me those butterfly eggs are caterpillars, and that caterpillars stop crawling and grow wings and become butterflies. Lark, you are too wise to believe such nonsense yourself, for you know it is *impossible*."

"I know no such thing," the lark said. "Whether I hover over the fields or go high up into the sky, I see many wonderful things. I know of no reason why there should not be more. Oh, caterpillar, it is only because you crawl, because you never get beyond your patch of cabbages, that you call these things impossible,"

"Nonsense," the caterpillar shouted in as loud a voice as she could manage. "I know what's possible and what's not possible – just as well as you do. Look at my long body and these rows of legs, and then talk to me about having *wings*. You foolish bird!"

"And *you* are a foolish caterpillar," the indignant lark replied. "You are foolish to attempt to argue about things you cannot understand. Do you not hear how my song swells with joy whenever I visit the mysterious wonder-world above? Oh, caterpillar, I have been there and returned. Trust me when I tell you these things."

"That is what you call . . ."

"Faith," the lark interrupted.

"And how am I to learn faith?" the caterpillar asked.

At that moment she felt something by her side. She looked round. Eight little green caterpillars like herself were moving about, and had already made a hole in the leaf of the cabbage. They had broken from the butterfly's eggs.

Shame and amazement filled the caterpillar's heart, but delight soon followed. If this was possible, perhaps she really would become a butterfly one day.

"Teach me your lesson, lark," she said, and the lark sang

A Lesson of Faith

to her of the wonders of the earth below, and of the heavens above. The caterpillar talked day after day to her relatives and friends of the time when she would become a butterfly.

But none of them believed her. Nevertheless, she had learned the lark's lesson of faith. When she was going into her chrysalis, she said, "I shall be a butterfly some day."

But her relatives thought her head was wandering, and said, "Poor thing."

She said quietly, "I have known many wonders. I have faith. I can trust even now for what shall come next."

Epilogue on page 119

Chris Wright

THE ROCKY ISLAND
Samuel Wilberforce

I saw in a dream a rough and rocky island rising straight up from a roaring sea. In the middle of the island rose a steep, black mountain. Dark clouds hid the top of this mountain from sight, while deep red flames from a volcano lit up the clouds from time to time. Angry lightning and thunder tore at the few trees that grew on the mountain, and sometimes one would be smashed to pieces and crash down into the sea.

My first thoughts were that the island was completely deserted, for who would want to live on such a wild and frightening place? Then to my surprise I saw a beach covered with soft white sand, and on this beach were young people at play. They ran here and there – some collecting shells, others picking bright orange berries from the bushes that grew below the cliffs. A few raced towards

The Rocky Island

the water in fun, running back quickly as the waves rushed up the sands towards them.

One boy began calling to the seabirds. The birds stood watching as he crept close, holding out a hand. Then they hopped away, but did not seem to feel themselves in any danger. A loud roar from the top of the mountain sent huge flames high into the clouds, and I was amazed how little concern the young people seemed to have for the dangers that surrounded them.

As the roar from the mountain got louder, they paused in their play. Then the thunder crashed closer than ever, making everyone run together into a frightened group. Soon the thunder died away, and before long all was forgotten and the young people started their games once more.

For some time I stood and watched. Then to my surprise a man appeared. He walked slowly along the beach, calling to everyone by name to gather round him. His face was kind, and his voice gentle.

"Listen to me," I heard him say. "I have come to show you the way to a safer and happier place than this. I am the prince of a land that is far away. My father the king wishes me to take you safely to him. Believe me, you must not remain here any longer."

They listened to the prince quietly, and then turned to each other. "How can we get away?" I heard one boy whisper to another. "We'll never be able to swim across the sea. I think we ought to stay and risk the dangers of the mountain."

The prince heard what was whispered, and stooped down to the boy. "Do not stay here," he warned in a firm but loving voice. "You certainly cannot swim to safety, but I have made a way of escape. Follow me, and you will see."

The prince led everyone past a high rock to another beach. Here the sea was calm, rippling gently among a fleet of small, brightly colored sailing boats, each large enough for just one person. There was a rudder to steer with, a pure white sail to carry the boat along its course, and at the top of each mast a white flag with a cross of bright red. The flags and the sails fluttered in the breeze.

When the young people saw these boats they looked at each other in excitement, but the prince held out a hand in warning. "The voyage will be difficult," he said. "At times the sea will be stormy and dangerous. But you need not be afraid, for although at times the waves may be high and frightening, I am leading you to a wonderful land where there is no angry mountain. There will be trees by the side of a beautiful river, and the trees will always be green and the leaves always fresh. The fruits on the trees will ripen every month. There is happiness and light there for ever."

The prince paused to make sure everyone was listening. "There are others there who have passed safely over this sea. Some of you will find fathers and mothers, and brothers and sisters. I shall look after you during the voyage, and be with you always."

As soon as the prince finished speaking, everyone was anxious to be on their way. As he helped each of the young people into their boats, the prince told them they must never look back at the rocky island, but must keep their eyes open for the wonderful land where they were going. If they had any shells or berries with them they must leave them behind. If they tried to take these with them in the boats, they would soon be in difficulty.

When some of them heard these instructions they crept away, then ran quickly back to the beach where they had just been playing. Then to my surprise I thought I could see others hiding shells and berries in their pockets, before jumping into their boats and pretending they had left everything behind.

The prince had gifts for everyone in the boats. First there was a compass hidden inside a special book. "You will each have one of these," he said, "and you must study it closely. Then you will know the way to steer as you follow me across the water. When the darkness of night comes on, or a thick mist surrounds you, or there is no breeze to help you on your way, you may not be able to see me. It is then that you must open your books and look at your compass, and its needle will always point true and straight to where I am."

There was another present for everybody: a musical pipe

that gave out a soft, murmuring sound when blown gently. "Playing on this is like talking to me," the prince said. "You can make use of it as often as you wish, even when things are going well. It will help the voyage pass easily. And be very sure to use it to call me when your boat will not keep on course, or when the waves are large and frightening. Then I will be with you to help you."

The young people took their gifts and stowed them securely in their boats. As they sailed away from the rocky island I thought how wonderful everything looked. The snow-white sails stood out brightly against the blue of the sea like specks of white floating in the sky, but the sea on the other side of the island looked dark and stormy. Everyone followed the prince. So far, they all seemed to be finding the voyage easy.

Then as I watched I could see some boats dropping behind, although most stayed close to the prince. A few were even going off course to the right or the left.

At first I was puzzled that they should be drifting away so soon. Then I could see many reasons for this. In one boat a girl kept turning to look at the island that had been her

The Rocky Island

home. She seemed to have forgotten the prince's warning. While she turned to look, her boat drifted further and further back towards the rocky island.

Then the sound of her friends who had chosen to stay behind came clearly across the waves. They seemed to be having such fun that the girl forgot the burning mountain and the dangers. She forgot the land of safety she had been so excited to set course for in the boat. She forgot the prince who had promised to be with her through all difficulties. As she listened to the others playing on the sand, a wave lifted her boat and carried it onto some rocks close to the shore.

I turned in disappointment, and saw two other boats keeping close together, but for some reason going faster and faster away from the true course. Then I realized the boys were having an angry race. They were so busy trying to get the better of each other that they forgot to look for the prince's boat, or to watch the finger of the compass. The more they tried to race, the further they went in the wrong direction.

There was another boat that was also going the wrong way. This time there was no one at the rudder to steer the correct course. The girl was playing with something in the bottom of the boat. Then I saw she had some of the bright orange berries they had been warned to leave behind.

As I watched, her boat too was carried onto a rock with such force that a hole was ripped in its side, and it began to sink.

Surely the boats following the prince closely would make me happier to watch. Here I was puzzled by the way one boat would be sailing along in calm water, while another close to it was battling through a sudden storm.

One boat became surrounded by a heavy darkness. The boy in it called out to his friends, and in answer they told him to play some music. When he blew softly on his pipe I knew he was safe again. But sometimes the darkness seemed too much to call through, and several boats became lost in silence.

In spite of the darkness, the young sailors only had to read the compass that was inside their book, and the needle would light up to show the way. Then they would blow on their pipes, and the darkness lifted as the music rose softly from their boats. At times like this I thought the young sailors could more clearly see the beautiful land the prince had told them about, than they could see their friends sailing close by.

Then I noticed another boat that had stopped moving altogether. The boat and its sail were so still they could have been part of a painted picture. The wind and the waves had gone. It was strange that another boat shot along close by, its sail blowing out full in a fresh breeze. But the boat that lay in the calm water showed no sign of movement.

I saw this happen to many boats along the way. If the

The Rocky Island

young sailors sat in the bottom of their boats and left their compass and pipe alone, the boats lay still until night came. However, if they picked up the tuneful instrument and blew gently into it, the soft music seemed to whisper to the wind, and suddenly the blood-red cross of the flag would lift itself over the water and the sail would fill with a fresh breeze. Before long the boat would be dancing on its way.

I watched other boats that were going well, but would suddenly come to a stormy patch of water. Great waves lifted up their angry white heads, but on each side the sea was calm. Quickly the young sailors would look ahead for signs of the prince, and get out the compass. If the way led through the stormy water they would need a bold heart and a faithful hand to steer straight ahead. But always, just when the water seemed to be at its most dangerous, the waves would die down and let their boats pass through in safety. Then the wind would blow the boats faster than before to the distant land.

How different for the sailor who decided not to trust the compass. One boy had been getting on well until now, but the sight of the raging waves frightened him. For a time he kept his boat going straight ahead, but then turned at the last moment into a patch of calm. Then, when all seemed to be well, a hidden sandbank caught his boat and held it fast.

Another boy followed this boat. This seemed to happen often. Whenever one boat went off course, others would follow it, the sailors forgetting to read their compass and test the way. And so it happened now. The boy who was following, suddenly saw the sandbank and tried to turn aside, but too late. The water became rough, and tipped the small boat onto its side.

I was glad to see three or four boats getting along safely together. Ever since leaving the rocky island they had stayed with each other. Few others had got on so well in their voyage. I could see, as I looked closely at their faces, that they were all one family. All through the voyage they kept cheering each other up, and helping first one and then another through difficulties. If one of them got into some sort of trouble with the boat, the others would come over to help. Instead of being slowed down by this, they seemed to get along faster and easier on their journey.

I realized that the voyage that to me seemed short, had really been long – a lifetime. Many of the sailors who had set out as young people were now much older. I longed to see how each voyage would end. So I stayed with the boat that was furthest forward, so I could watch it come to land.

First this boat, and then the ones that followed, came to an area of storm and darkness just before the shore of the happy land. True, some of the boats found the storm and the darkness easier than did others, but every boat had to pass alone through this part of the sea. Even the family that had been so close to each other had to separate when they

The Rocky Island

reached this dark part.

"Peace," the prince called to each boat as it entered the storm. "Do not be troubled." But some of the sailors, especially the older ones, chose to ignore his voice as they tried to find their own way through.

The boats that sailed in fastest seemed to get through the best. Indeed, this happened every time. When the sailor kept an eye on the compass, and held tightly to the rudder, the storm and darkness caused little trouble. Others would play soft music as they passed through.

Then the boat would break through into the brightness of the land that lay beyond. The joyful sound of family and friends, gathered on the shore to greet them, drifted across the water.

There were others waiting there, too, who were like people and yet they were different – as only seen in some dream of angels. These were their friends too, for they welcomed them on the shore. Then the sailors were lifted up and carried with songs of triumph into the shining presence of the king.

There, sitting on a royal throne beside his father, they saw the prince wearing a glorious crown. Each person smiled up at the face of gentle majesty that had first looked on them when they played on the shore of that now distant island, so long ago. They heard again the voice that had urged them to flee from the burning mountain.

This was the prince who had given them a boat and told them to follow him; the prince who had been near them through the storms; who had given them light in the darkness and helped them through the times when their boats had been halted by the calm. They saw the king's son who had never left them; who had kept and guided them across the ocean – through the final storm and darkness – and who now received them, young and old, to his never-ending rest.

Epilogue on page 121

WAITING
Margaret Gatty

The house crickets must have led a sorry life before people built houses with fireplaces; before there were kitchen hearths with warm nooks in the corners where they could sing their cheerful songs, coming out every now and then to bask in the glow of the comforting fire.

There was a time when the house crickets had no place to shelter, except in hollow trees, or cracks in rocks and stones, or some equally gloomy place. Besides all this, they had to put up with the mockery of creatures who were perfectly comfortable themselves, and so could not understand their lack of cheerfulness.

"Why don't you go and jump and sing in the fields with your cousins the grasshoppers?" a spider once complained as she tried to twist her web in a hole in a wall where she found a house cricket hiding. "I'm sure your legs are long enough – if you'd only take the trouble to unbend them. The trouble with you and your family is that you all keep moping in corners like this, when you should be outside leaping about and enjoying yourselves. And I dare say your family could sing a lot more loudly – if you only put your minds to it."

Now this was such a long speech for a busy spider to make, that the house cricket felt perhaps he ought to take notice. Something, he decided, must be very wrong with him, but what that something was he had no idea. All the other creatures seemed contented. The spider, for instance, was quite at home in the hole *he* found so dismal. The flies, the bees, the ants were satisfied with life – as was the mole who sometimes came up from burrowing to tell wonderful stories of his underground delights.

The cricket thought of the birds with their joyful songs, the huge beasts that walked about like giants in the fields – they all seemed happy enough. Every one of them had the home he liked, and no one was jealous of the other.

But with the house crickets it was exactly the opposite. They never felt at home anywhere. It always seemed to them that they were looking for something that was not there, some place that could never be found, some situation where they could be at peace at last.

This cricket knew he was built for energy, yet he felt compelled to live in dark holes. Yes, he could make music, but few had ever heard him make it. Life for him was just one long complaint.

Waiting

Often he would meet with other house crickets and talk the matter over. They looked at their long folded-up legs, and as far as they could see they were exactly like the legs of their cousins the grasshoppers. Yet the idea of jumping about in the grass all day long filled them with horror. One day an unusually brave cricket decided to go out into the big field and talk to the grasshoppers about their problems.

The first grasshopper he saw agreed to go back with him and see if he could offer any help. Perhaps, he said, the crickets were unwell, or had been badly looked after when they were young and had suffered some damage to their legs.

The crickets were waiting in the foot of a hollow tree where they had taken shelter, and the grasshopper got there ahead of the cricket for he went along in great leaps and bounds. In fact, he arrived so suddenly that the waiting crickets were taken aback by what they called impolite behavior.

Carefully the grasshopper examined the crickets' legs and knees. He pulled their legs straight, for he thought there might be some fault in the way they were put together. But he could find nothing amiss. He could see all the crickets sitting there, with their legs and bodies as nicely made as his own, yet the crickets had no energy for jumping.

But before he could give his findings, he was overcome with the fidgets, and said, "You must excuse me, my cousins, for I have cramp in my left leg. I must jump."

And jump he did: once, twice, three times, and was out of the tree. Whether on purpose or by accident, he kept jumping and was never seen again.

One day the mole emerged from one of his tunnels beside the hollow tree, and heard the crickets complaining about life.

"What is the use of all this grumbling?" he asked them, when he had heard enough. "You admit that every other creature is perfect in its way, and happy."

The crickets said they agreed.

"Well then," the mole continued, "I am quite sure you are perfect in your way too, although you have not yet found out your purpose in life. One day I am certain you will discover why you are made as you are."

The crickets asked the mole if he knew what he was talking about, for it seemed extremely unlikely to them that they could have any reason for living.

"Listen to me," the mole said patiently. "Have you ever thought what it must be like for a young mole when he first begins to burrow in the earth? Do you think he knows why he's doing it? It's a complete working in the dark." The mole paused here for the crickets to smile at his joke, but they just stared at him.

"Dear me," the mole said, "can you imagine what a hardship it must be to drive your nose into the ground, hour after hour, without having any idea why you are doing it? I remember it well myself. We pushed the earth away until we had formed a perfect underground palace. And the worms and grubs we found along the way . . ." The mole paused and licked his lips. "Well, I really must be going."

"No, wait," the crickets called. "If we knew what purpose *we* have in life, then we would gladly do it. As it is, we have *nothing* to do."

"It's nonsense to talk of having nothing to do," the mole said. "Think about what you already do each day. In the morning you hunt for the sunny places because they are warm. In the evening you search for small hiding places for shelter."

"And what's the use of that?" one cricket asked rudely.

"Ah," the mole said, "on the farm near here there was once a young ox. As soon as he could run about he kept banging his clumsy head against everything he met. None of us could tell why, and many of our friends were much offended by what they thought was his lack of manners. The farm dogs were much amused, and used to bark at him – even close to him at times – as he lowered his head to them."

The crickets looked at each other and yawned. They could think of no reason why the mole was telling them this story.

"Well," the mole went on, ignoring the crickets' rudeness, "the secret came out at last. Two fine horns grew out of the head of that young ox, and everyone understood the reason for all the butting. Except the farm dogs. One of them was playing the old barking game, and got firmly tossed into the air for his pains. So you see, everything fits in at last, my friends, even if it means waiting."

The crickets realized they had been fortunate that the mole had given them this advice, for a fox had recently suggested they should all starve themselves to death and put an end to their whole miserable race, for he had agreed with the crickets that they seemed to serve no useful purpose in the world.

But the mole's good sense gave them a different view on life, and from that time on hope grew in their hearts until it created a sort of happiness in itself. So they decided to wait, but in the meantime they continued to watch for the warm sun in the morning, as their friend the mole had advised.

In the evenings they hid in small hollows in trees and walls, and told each other stories of their early ancestors who had traveled around the world, preferring hot countries. There was a rumor that a cricket family had discovered a sort of dreamland at the mouth of a volcano, but no one had ever returned from there to say that this was true, for they were doubtless swept away at the first eruption that took place.

The crickets knew of ancestors who searched out fires made by early human hands. Some of these fires were built by wanderers in forests, others were made by dwellers in tents. Whenever news of a new fire spread, the crickets had hurried there, but too late. The travelers had moved on and put the fires out.

"Now," the crickets agreed, when they had finished retelling their family history, "we must do as the mole says, and wait."

Then one of the crickets sang in a high-pitched voice, "Everything will be perfect at last. There is a reason why we are here." And the others joined in as loudly as they could.

The day they were all waiting for arrived at long last. People came and built houses. Inside the houses they made chimneys, and in each hearth they put a flat stone. In these dwellings all the doubts and woes of the crickets' lives were over. The waiting seemed like a dream that faded into nothing. Oh, what joy the crickets felt. How loudly they shouted, how high they sprang.

"Mole was right," they sang. "Everything is perfect now, for no one could be as happy as we are."

"Grandmother," they heard a young girl ask an old woman sitting by the hearth, "what is that I hear singing so loudly in the corner?"

"I do not hear it, my dear," the old woman answered, "for my hearing is poor. But if something is singing, then it must be happy and enjoying the warmth of this fire as much as I am. You know what the Good Book says: 'Let everything that has breath praise the Lord.'"

So it is no wonder that round those warm and friendly fires no voice is louder, no voice more joyful, than that of the house cricket. Now at last the crickets knew why they had been born as they were. There was a point to their lives after all, but it took the wisdom of the mole to explain it to them.

Some say crickets bring a blessing to the family around whose hearth they settle. And in a way they do, for they bring with them a tale of promises made good. They sing a song of hope rewarded, even though in that happy sound there is neither speech nor language that we can recognize. Yet they have found their answer to the question that so many ask – why am I here?

Epilogue on page 123

THE WANDERERS
Samuel Wilberforce

In a filthy hut, built on the edge of a bleak hillside, a poor widow lived with her two sons. She dressed them in torn and dirty rags because she had nothing better for them to wear. Often the boys were hungry and cold, for she had little food.

The boys had not learnt to read and write, because their mother did not know one letter from another. When they went out to play, the only friends they met were as poorly dressed as they were, for this was a desolate place in which to be born and live.

One day their mother was taken seriously ill with a fever. No one knew she was ill, except her two sons, and they had no one to turn to for help.

After a week the widow died, leaving her two sons all alone. As they sat outside their hut crying, a man passing by asked the boys why they were so sad. Quickly they explained about their mother.

Immediately the man called to his servant who was with him and arranged for the widow to be buried. "And now you must come with me," he told the two boys. "The king is my father, and I will take care of you."

With this, he led the widow's sons to a beautiful castle where he made sure the dirt was washed away, before dressing them in the finest clothes instead of their rags.

"I want you to belong to my family," the man told them, "and I will give you new names." He touched the older brother on the shoulder. "You are now called Leo, which means Lion, for I want you to be brave and bold." Then he took the hand of the other brother. "And you are now Zimri, which means Homeland, for this is your home now. Come and have some good food."

After Leo and Zimri had eaten the best food they had ever tasted, the king's son introduced them to the many other young people living with him in the castle. They quickly became friends. For the first time in their lives the boys felt happy.

Sometimes Leo and Zimri spent their time exploring the castle, and sometimes they played with their new friends in the huge garden. Here they discovered all sorts of flowers, wonderful trees full of singing birds, and brightly painted butterflies flitting from place to place. They were more contented than they had ever imagined could be possible.

When Leo and Zimri had been in the castle for a few weeks, and were getting bolder, the king's son walked over to them and put his hands on their shoulders. "I have come to give you a warning," he said. "As you may have seen, my garden ends at the edge of a vast wilderness."

"We've seen it," Leo said, "but there's no reason for us to go there. It looks a terrible place."

"It is indeed a terrible place," the king's son said. "My enemy lives out there, and wants nothing more than to capture those who live here with me."

Zimri clung tightly to the king's son when he heard this. "Will you keep us safe?" he asked.

The man held onto both boys. "No harm can come to you while you stay here with me," he assured them. "You are in no danger – unless you cross the line that marks the end of my garden"

Later that day the boys asked their friends if it really was dangerous to cross the line and enter the wilderness. A girl called Belle said she knew of several young people who had crossed the line. Once there, the enemy had seized them.

"Where are they now?" Zimri asked.

Belle looked sad. "I believe they are slaves in the enemy's castle," she said.

"Didn't they see the line?" Leo asked. "Why would anyone want to cross it?"

"The enemy is cunning," Belle explained. "He lays out flowers just the other side of the line. Some of them look even more beautiful than the flowers here. But when one of us tries to get them, they lose their color. But just a bit further into the wilderness there are even more beautiful flowers. And when these too lose their color, there are more – just a bit further away again. And then the enemy pounces."

Leo shook his head. "That is something I will *never* do," he boasted. "You can be sure the enemy will never capture *me* like that."

Zimri stayed silent as he thought of the young people who had been taken into slavery in the wilderness. "Then I must always be careful," he said quietly.

A few days later Zimri noticed his brother going very close to the wilderness. Leo laughed and said he was only having a look, and was certainly not going to cross the line.

"It's strange," Leo said. "When I was close to the castle, the flowers on the other side of the line looked dry and colorless, but now I'm closer they seem to grow brighter and brighter. I wonder why."

He went right up to the line and noticed that although the flowers close to the line were already fading, there seemed to be a whole carpet of brightly colored flowers covering the ground as far as the eye could see, just as Belle had said. But his brother Zimri persuaded Leo to return to the castle.

The next day Leo was running to hide in a game he was playing with Zimri, when he came unexpectedly to the line marking the start of the wilderness – the line the king's son had warned them they must never cross. At that moment he caught sight of something bright and shiny among the carpet of flowers, and jumped across the line to see what it could be.

As Leo crossed the line he heard his brother Zimri shouting at him, and in panic he returned to the safety of the castle garden. Leo looked pale when he thought back over what he had just done. He said he could feel his legs shake at the thought of his fortunate escape, and for a time he sat quietly under a tree to recover from his fright.

The next day Leo again found himself near the line, and looked once more for the bright and shiny object. After all, he told himself, he had crossed the line yesterday and managed to get back safely. Surely he could do it again – as long as he only went a short way and kept the castle in sight. He begged his younger brother to cross with him.

At first Zimri shook his head, but when his older brother assured him they would be perfectly safe, he at last agreed to go just a little way into the wilderness. As they crossed the line, very carefully, a brightly colored bird rose up from under their feet. The boys had never seen such a bird. All the colors of the rainbow shone from its feathers, and its black and scarlet head seemed to sparkle in the sunshine.

Instead of flying, it ran in front of Leo and Zimri, flapping its wings as though trying to lead them to a better place.

The boys were soon in full chase, and everything else was forgotten. The bird let them keep close, and they never noticed how far they were getting from the safety of the castle garden. They heard their friend Belle calling to them, but her voice sounded faint and they had more far exciting things to do than listen to her.

Suddenly the sand rose like a cloud, and the sound of galloping horses filled their ears. All they could see in the dust were occasional glimpses of horses and riders. The boys never thought to call out to the king's son as they clung to each other in panic.

Strong arms reached down and seized them, and Leo and Zimri knew they were in the hands of the enemy. In another minute they were strapped to the back of a horse, racing off to the dwelling of the enemy.

The boys cried and begged to be taken home, but in vain. They were told to stay silent. They would be kept as slaves. Further and further the horses galloped, taking the two brothers away from the safety of the king's son. They could see no flowers laid out in a carpet now, no brightly colored bird, only a wilderness of rocks and sand where nothing grew. Ahead was the stronghold where the enemy lived, with iron bars at the windows to keep the prisoners inside.

The Wanderers

Zimri thought of the king's son, how he had rescued them from a place as dismal as this, and how he had promised them safety if they did not stray out of the garden. Zimri looked at his brother, but to his surprise Leo smiled and seemed no longer to care that he was a prisoner.

Just at that moment Zimri realized that the strap that bound him to the horse had grown loose. In a moment he slipped from the saddle and fell to the ground, hitting his head on a rock. No one noticed him fall, and for a long time he lay there unconscious, almost lifeless.

When he came to, the sound of the horses had died away and the sand that their hooves had disturbed had settled. He could see no trace of their tracks, and had no idea of the way back to the king's son. Wherever he looked, he could see only sand and rocks, baked by a scorching sun high overhead.

Zimri called for his brother, but got no answer. He staggered to his feet as the sun beat down on his head. His tongue felt dry and swollen from lack of water. He dropped to his knees, ready to die.

He thought again of the king's son, of Belle who had

shouted an urgent warning after he crossed the line with Leo – his brother who was probably already a slave in the terrible castle of the enemy. And now here he was, dying in this desolate place. He called to the king's son, but his voice was so weak that it seemed unlikely he would be heard. Even so, he cried out several times.

As Zimri closed his eyes he thought he could hear someone calling his name. But perhaps it was all in his mind, confusion brought on by the fall. He heard the voice again, and it certainly sounded like someone calling his name. He remembered how his friends had often told him the king's son was unwilling for any of them to be taken prisoner. Through his cracked lips he continued to call to the king's son, begging him to come to his rescue.

Suddenly a shadow fell across his blistered face. He looked up to see the king's son blocking out the hot sun, standing with a welcoming smile. Zimri recalled the same look on that face when the man had come to their filthy hut after their mother died. He had rescued them then, and taken them to live in his castle, and given them new clothes and good food.

The man reached out his hands and took Zimri in his arms. Zimri thought he could hear horses' hooves in the distance, but he knew he was safe, for no enemy would dare come close now. He had never felt such comfort as the king's son carried him safely over the scorching wilderness and set him down carefully in the shelter of the castle.

Belle and his other friends were there to welcome him, but Zimri hung his head in shame. Then, as he looked up into the face of the king's son, he could see great warmth, mixed with kindness and love. Tears rolled down his cheeks as he thought of his disobedience, and how the king's son had loved him so much that he had come to his rescue when he called out.

Zimri was washed tenderly, and king's son rubbed healing ointment onto his blistered face.

"My brother Leo isn't here," Zimri said at last. "Will you rescue him, too?"

The king's son looked sad. "You called out to me for help, Zimri. I cannot rescue people who do not call out to me."

"Leo has not called out to you?" As Zimri put the question he remembered how Leo had seemed almost happy to be taken prisoner. "Has he?" he asked.

The king's son shook his head.

As the days and months, then the years went on, Zimri and Belle often watched to see if Leo would be carried back safely to the castle. In the end they thought maybe he was dead, or perhaps had become one of the enemy's servants and was waiting out there in the wilderness, ready to snatch anyone who was foolish enough to leave the safety of the garden, looking for what they thought were even better things.

But Zimri never stopped thanking the king's son that he had heard him call out when he was taken captive by the enemy. He had been rescued by the great love of the mighty and merciful king's son. Maybe, one day, his brother Leo would call for help too. And if he did, surely the king's son would run to him and carry him back safely in his loving arms.

Epilogue on page 125

NOT LOST, BUT GONE BEFORE!
Margaret Gatty

"I wonder what becomes of the frog when he climbs up out of this world and disappears. Does anybody know where he goes?" The dragonfly nymph asked his companions this question a hundred times a day, as he darted through the woodland pond in search of food.

"Who cares where the frog goes?" one of the nymphs snapped. "What is it to us?"

"Look out for food for yourself," cried another, "and leave other people's business alone."

"But I really want to know," the nymph explained. "I followed a frog just now, and he began to disappear as soon as he reached the edge of the pond, and then he was gone. Did he leave this world, do you think? If so, what can there be beyond?"

"You idle, talkative fellow," cried another nymph, shooting by as he spoke. "Keep your mind on the world you're in, and leave the 'beyond' – if there is a 'beyond' – alone. See what a meal you've just missed with all your wonderings about nothing." So saying, the speaker seized a small grub that was swimming right in front of his friend.

But do what he would, the nymph could not help thinking of the curious disappearance of the frog, and presently began to bother his companions about it yet again. "Somebody has to tell me. What becomes of the frog when he leaves this world?"

The minnows passed by without speaking, for they knew no more about it than he did, but were not going to show their ignorance. The eels wriggled away, for they were always cross and could not bear to be disturbed.

The nymph grew impatient, and at last persuaded several of his friends to share his curiosity. They all went scrambling about, asking the same question of every creature they met. "What becomes of the frog when he leaves this world?"

Suddenly there was a heavy splash in the water, and a large green and yellow frog swam down to the bottom of the pond.

"Ask the frog," a minnow suggested, as he darted by with a cheeky look in his eye.

The thing was much easier said than done, for the frog was a dignified sort of creature. The smaller creatures in the pond were a little afraid of him, and it took a great amount of courage to ask someone as important as a frog where he had been, and where he had come from.

Still, such a chance of hearing his question answered was not to be lost, and after taking two or three turns round the roots of a water lily, the dragonfly nymph screwed up his courage. Approaching the frog nervously, he asked, "Is it permitted for a very unhappy creature to speak?"

The frog turned his gold-edged eyes on him in surprise, and answered, "If you're unhappy it might be better if you said nothing, for *I* only talk when I'm happy."

"But I *will* be happy – if you let me talk," the nymph said quickly.

"Talk away, then," the frog said.

"Respected frog," the nymph replied, "there is something I want to ask you."

"Yes?" the frog said – not in a very encouraging tone but, still, permission was given.

"What is there beyond the world?" the nymph asked, almost too quietly to be heard.

The frog rolled his goggle eyes round and round. "What world do you mean?"

"This world, of course. Our world." The nymph suddenly felt much bolder.

"Do you mean this *pond*?" the frog asked.

"I mean the place we live in, whatever you may choose to call it," cried the nymph. "I call it the world."

"Do you, sharp little fellow?" the frog said. "Then what is the place you don't live in, the 'beyond,' eh?" And he shook his sides with amusement as he spoke.

"That's just what I want you to tell me," the nymph replied quickly.

"Oh, indeed, little one!" The frog rolled his eyes again, this time with an amused twinkle. "Listen, and I will tell you. It is called dry land."

There was a pause of several seconds, and then, "Can I swim about there?" the nymph asked.

"I should think not," the frog chuckled. "Dry land isn't water, little fellow. That is just what it's *not*."

"But I want you to tell me what it *is*, not what it's *not*," the nymph persisted.

"Of all the inquisitive creatures I ever met, you certainly are the most troublesome," the frog said. "Well then, dry land is something like the mud at the bottom of this pond, only it is not wet, because there is no water."

"Really?" interrupted the nymph. "What's there, then?"

"That's the difficulty," the frog replied. "There *is* something there, of course, and they call it air. But you live here under the water, so I don't know how to explain air to you. I suppose it's the nearest possible thing to nothing. Do you understand?"

"Not quite," the nymph replied, hesitating.

"I was afraid of that. Now just take my advice," the frog urged, "and ask no more silly questions. No good can possibly come of it."

"Honored frog," the nymph replied, "I must disagree with you. I think *great* good will come of it, because right now I feel miserable and restless because I still don't know where you go when you leave the pond."

"Then you're a very silly fellow," the frog cried. "I tell you, the thing is not worth troubling yourself about. But, as I like your spirit – which, for so unimportant a creature, is astonishing – I will make you an offer. If you want to take a seat on my back, I will carry you up to dry land myself. Then you can judge for yourself what is there, and how you like it. I consider it a foolish experiment, and it will be entirely at your own risk."

"And I accept it with a gratitude that knows no bounds," the excited nymph exclaimed.

"Then climb on my back and cling to me as firmly as you can. For, remember, if you fall off you may be lost when I leave the water."

The nymph obeyed, and the frog swam gently upwards, reaching the bulrushes at the edge of the pond.

"Hold fast," he cried, and then raising his head out of the pond he clambered up the bank and sat on the grass.

"Now, then, here we are," he said. "What do you think of dry land?"

But no one spoke in reply.

"Hello? Gone?" he continued. "That's just what I was afraid of. He's floated off my back, stupid fellow. Dear, dear, how unlucky. But it cannot be helped. Perhaps he will make his way to the water's edge soon, and then I can help him out. I will come back later and see."

Away went the frog with an occasional merry leap along the grass at the edge of the pond, glancing every now and then among the bulrushes to see if he could spy the dark figure of the dragonfly nymph.

But the nymph, meanwhile? Ah, so far from having floated off the frog's back through carelessness, he had clung to it with hope, until the moment came when his face began to leave the water. But that same moment sent him shooting back into the pond, panting and struggling for life, and it was several seconds before he could recover himself.

"Horrible!" he cried as soon as he felt a little better. "Beyond this world there is nothing but death. The frog has deceived me. Wherever he goes, it cannot be *there*."

With these words, the nymph went back to his family and friends at the bottom of the pond, to tell them what he had done and where he had been. The hope, the mystery, the danger, the all-but-deadly result – and the still unexplained wonder of what happened to the frog when he left the only world they knew. The nymph soon had a host of followers, questioning and chattering at his heels.

That evening the inquisitive nymph was returning from a swim among the water plants when he suddenly encountered, sitting silently on a stone at the bottom of the pond, his friend the green and yellow frog.

"You there!" the nymph cried. "You never left this world at all! And to think I was foolish enough to trust you!"

"You puzzle me by your unpleasant remarks," the frog replied. "However, I forgive you. You are so ignorant that good manners cannot reasonably be expected from you, little fellow. It never struck you, I suppose, to think what my thoughts were when I landed on the grass and discovered you were no longer on my back. Why didn't you sit tightly as I told you?"

"You're being most unfair," the angry nymph exclaimed.

"Not so," the frog said. "It is always the way with you foolish fellows who think they can understand everything. The first difficulty you meet and you give up."

They were on the point of quarrelling, and would certainly have done so had not the frog, with unusual kindness, asked the nymph to tell his own story.

It was soon told. The frog stared in silence out of his great goggle eyes while the nymph went through the details of his terrible adventure.

"And now," the nymph said, "as it's clear there is nothing beyond this world but death, all your stories of going there must be make-believe. So, if you do leave this world at all, you must go to some other place you are unwilling to tell me about. You have a right to your secret, I admit, but as I have no wish to be tricked by any more travelers' tales, I will bid you a very good evening."

"You will do no such thing," the frog said firmly. "Not until you have listened as carefully to my story as I have done to yours."

Then he told how he had remained by the edge of the pond in the vain hope of seeing the nymph; how he had hopped about in the grass; how he had peeped among the bulrushes. "And at last," he continued, "though I did not see you, I saw a sight that I believe has more interest for you than for any other creature that lives." And there he paused.

"And what was that?" the inquisitive nymph asked, his interest returning.

"Up the polished green stalk of one of those bulrushes I saw a nymph, just like yourself, slowly climbing until he left the water behind him. He was clinging firmly to the reed, with the sun shining brightly on his body. Considering the fondness you nymphs show for the shady bottom of the pond, I was very surprised. So I continued to watch. Presently your friend's body started to break open."

"What nonsense you talk!" the nymph interrupted rudely.

"Do you want me to tell this story or not?" the frog asked loudly. "What I am saying is the truth."

The nymph drew back slightly. "Most noble frog, I did not mean to insult you. But it seems . . ."

"I know what I saw," the frog said firmly. "Your friend's body started to break open. And after many struggles what do you think came out?"

The nymph just shook his head and said nothing. The frog seemed to be talking nonsense, but he was not going to tell him so.

"Very well, I will tell you," the frog continued. "It was one of those magnificent creatures I have often seen floating through the air above this pond. They dazzle my eyes as they pass so quickly. It had become . . . a glorious . . . *dragonfly*!"

The nymph stared, filled with a mixture of wonder and disbelief.

"Then he lifted his wings out of the casing," the frog continued, "and although they were shriveled and damp at first, the wings stretched and expanded in the sunshine until they glistened like fire."

The frog closed his large eyes as though seeing the sight again in his mind.

"After a while I saw the beautiful creature suddenly take flight, and four long wings flashed back the sunshine. I heard the sharp noise with which they struck the air, and I saw his body give out rays of glittering blue and green as he darted along. And away, away he flew over the water in circles that seemed to know no end. And now I have come here to tell you about it."

"It's a wonderful story," the nymph observed at last, with less excitement than might have been expected.

"A wonderful story, indeed," the frog repeated. "May I ask your opinion about it?"

"First tell me what *you* think," the nymph answered politely.

"Good. You are ready to listen at last," the frog remarked. "Well then, I believe the world up there will one day belong to you."

"That is possible – if your account is true," the nymph said, with a doubtful air.

"Little fellow," the frog exclaimed, "I know what I saw."

"And you really think that the glorious creature you describe was once a . . ."

"Silence!" the frog cried. "I am not prepared to discuss the matter any further. Goodbye. It will soon be night, and I am returning to my grassy home on dry land. Go to rest, little fellow, and live in hope."

The frog swam to the bank and clambered up its side, while the nymph returned to his tribe which was already preparing to rest during the hours of darkness.

As the days passed, the inquisitive nymph began to feel different inside. His limbs grew tired, and a strange feeling came over him. The water in which he had been born now felt choking. Perhaps, after all, the frog had spoken the truth.

His friends and relations gathered round. Some were his age, but many were much younger. They asked him to promise that if there really was a world beyond their own, he would return and tell them so. The nymph readily agreed.

"But if you should forget!" one of the younger generation exclaimed, timid and uneasy.

"Forget the old home, my friend?" the nymph asked. "Forget our life of enjoyment here, the excitement of the chase for food, the triumph of success? Forget the feelings of hope and fear we have shared together? Impossible!"

"But you may not be *able* to come back to us," another nymph suggested.

"More unlikely still," the exhausted nymph murmured. "Goodbye, my friends, you need have no fears for me. I shall return and tell you all about the life out there."

"You will remember your promise?" one of his best friends called out.

"I will," he replied.

"Faithfully?" the first speaker urged.

"Solemnly."

The nymph sounded weak. Slowly he rose through the

water to the reeds and bulrushes at the edge of the pond. Two favorite brothers and a few of his friends, more adventurous than the rest, went with him, hoping to see whatever might take place. But as the nymph climbed higher, they were disappointed.

Eyes made for the water were unable to see the world beyond. The little group returned in sorrow to the bottom of the pond.

The sun was high in the heavens when the dragonfly nymph departed from his friends, and they waited through the long hours of the day for his return – first in hope, then in sadness as the shades of evening began to deepen.

"He has forgotten us," some cried.

"Something terrible and final has happened to him," others said.

"He will return to us yet," maintained the few who clung to hope.

But, in vain, messenger after messenger shot upwards to the foot of the bulrushes and to various parts of the pond, hoping to discover some trace of the lost nymph. All returned in sorrow.

When day came, and the sun sent its rays of light to the bottom of the pond, the nymphs awoke in bitter disappointment. The frog had not told the truth.

"We used to get along perfectly well without thinking about such things," they said. "But to have great hopes held out, and to be deceived by the frog – it is more than we can be expected to bear."

Then, with rage that nothing could hold back, they chased their prey with a terrible anger in their search for food.

By the end of the second day they decided to stop grieving openly for the one they had loved, but on the morning of the third day one of the nymph's favorite brothers joined his companions as they were preparing to start their daily life of searching for food. They noticed that his eyes stood out as they had never stood out before.

"My friends," he said, "I was, as you know, one of our lost relative's favorite brothers. I trusted him, but he has not returned to us."

The favorite brother paused, and a group in a corner murmured among themselves, "Why has he not returned? The story about that other world must be false."

"He has not returned to us," the favorite brother repeated, "but, my friends, I believe I am going to him, to that new life he spoke about. Something is making me want to go upwards, ever upwards. Before I leave you, I make the same solemn promise he made to you. Should the great hope be true, we will both come back and tell you so. Goodbye."

The nymph rose through the water, followed by the last of his brothers and one or two of the younger nymphs. On reaching the edge of the pond he caught hold of a reed, and clinging to its firm stalk he clambered into the open air.

The others watched as he left the water. But after that they saw him no more. They sank down, sad and uneasy, to their home below.

The hours of the day passed as before, and not a trace of the departed one was seen. For a time they held to the words he had spoken, the promise he had made. Their hope died with the setting sun, and many a voice was raised against his lack of love.

"He is faithless," some said.

"He has forgotten us, just like his brother did," cried others.

"The story about that other world is false," repeated the group in the corner.

Only a few said to each other, "We will not despair."

Another day passed and then, in the early dawn following, the third and last brother crept slowly to a sleepy group of his friends.

"Look at my eyes," he said. "Has a change come over them? To me, they feel swollen and bursting, and the world here looks cloudy and unclear. Some power I cannot see is driving me upwards, as the others were driven. Listen, then. Let the other world be what it will – gorgeous beyond all we can imagine, blissful beyond all we can hope for – I will not forget you. If it is possible, I shall return. Farewell!"

And he too went up through the cool water of the pond

to the plants that bordered its side. Then, from the leaf of a golden king-cup he clambered into the world of air, into which a nymph's eye never could pierce.

His companions stayed near the spot where he had disappeared, but neither sight nor sound came to them. Only the great sense of loss reminded them that he had once been there with them.

Then followed hours of waiting, more disappointment, cruel doubts, and hope mixed with despair. And after this, day by day other nymphs left the pond.

But among those who were left, the result was always the same. There were some who doubted and feared, some who disbelieved and made fun, and others who hoped and looked forward without worry.

If those eyes that worked so well under the water could have seen into the pure air above the pond, what a lifetime of anxiety many would have been spared. What peace, what joy could have been theirs.

And what of the first dragonfly nymph? Was he really faithless, as they thought? When he burst from his old body by the waterside and rose on glittering wings into the summer air, had he forgotten the ones so recently left behind? Had he no feelings for their griefs and fears? No memory of the promise he had made?

Far from it. He thought of them during the excitement of his wildest flights, and returned time after time to the edge of the pond that had once been the only world he knew. But now he could never return to the water.

The least touch on its surface as he skimmed over it brought on a deadly shock, like the shock he had experienced as a nymph on reaching the air on the back of the frog.

"Alas for the promise I made in ignorance, miserable nymph that I was," became his constantly repeated cry.

And thus apart yet joined by love, he hovered above the barrier of water that lay between them, always hoping that he would see his family and friends come into sight.

To his delight he was there to welcome the brother who followed him, and the brother who followed soon after that – not to a strange and friendless place, but to a home rich with welcome from those who had gone before.

And today, in the breezy air by the woodland pond, on a bright summer afternoon you can hear the clashing of dragonflies' wings, as now backwards, now forwards, now to one side, now to another, they dart over the crystal water in the adventure of their new life.

Epilogue on page 127

AGATHOS
Samuel Wilberforce

There once was a mighty king whose country was troubled by a fierce and deadly dragon. The king called his soldiers together, to send them to the place where the creature was causing so much trouble.

"You must be prepared to fight this dragon," he told his soldiers. "The prince, who is my son, has already fought with him and defeated him, even though he put forth all his rage and power against him. However, the dragon is not yet dead, and is still able to cause trouble. My strength shall go with you in battle, but you must always be on the lookout for danger."

The soldiers turned to each other but they felt no fear, for they trusted their king for everything.

"If you remember my words and call on my name in times of danger, I will be with you," the king promised. "Look, I have provided armor for you. Wear it boldly, and the dragon can never harm you. But if he finds you unprepared – if he attacks when you are not wearing this armor – he will certainly harm you. He may even defeat you."

The soldiers promised to be on their guard, and they set off in high spirits into the land where the dragon lay.

At first they were extremely careful to wear their armor. They never all slept at once, arranging for some to watch while others rested. It was a fine sight to see the king's soldiers marching up and down the land in their shining armor, and the people of the country felt safe because they were keeping guard.

Every morning the sleeping men would wake refreshed. Putting on their armor most carefully they called to their prince to keep them safe and loyal. Then they would go out to keep guard against the dragon, while their comrades came off duty to rest.

This was indeed a splendid sight, but alas it did not last. Never once did the soldiers see the dragon, and everything went on quietly around them. The farmers ploughed the land; the reapers went about to reap the harvest; there were marriages and feasts, and games and work.

The soldiers began to think that perhaps the story of the dragon was just that – a story. So they forgot their king's instructions to watch and stand fast. The weather grew hotter, and their armor seemed to grow heavier by the day.

"What is the use of this helmet?" one of them complained. "The sun heats it up until it scorches my head."

"You are right," a friend agreed. "Besides, no one ever *sees* this enemy. I'm leaving my helmet in the camp. There will be time enough to fetch it if I ever see the dragon coming."

Another soldier complained of the weight of his breastplate, and refused to wear it. Yet another decided that his shield was such a nuisance that he would put it in his tent – where he could surely reach it quickly in time of danger.

The thick sandals made the soldiers' feet uncomfortable. Finally they left them off and walked barefoot. It was pleasant to feel the soft earth beneath their feet.

Before long the soldiers were walking around the countryside with little of their armor to be seen. Their cool clothes were more sensible than those the king had provided – so they told each other.

Some went to this feast, while others went to that. It was hard to tell that the soldiers belonged to the king, for they could no longer be recognized by their armor.

But one soldier refused to change his ways. His name was Agathos. It saddened Agathos to see his comrades living so carelessly. Often he warned them that the enemy must surely be near, even though they never saw him.

"We know our prince fought the evil creature," he said.

"So surely the king knows how dangerous this enemy can be."

The other soldiers laughed at Agathos but he put up with their taunts, and neither their harsh words nor the hot sun made him weary. There was nothing anyone could do to make him take off the king's armor. At times his feet felt sore within his heavy sandals, but he knew they must have been given for a good reason. At other times he felt like sleeping when it was his turn to watch at night, but Agathos did what he had to do. He trusted the king and knew it was important to be ready at all times.

As the months passed, things became more and more difficult for Agathos. The words of his idle companions grew harsher as they became more and more certain that the dragon would never attack – if it existed at all.

But just when they thought themselves safe, the danger was suddenly at hand. One of the soldiers was returning to the camp from a great feast where there had been much merriment. He had decided his armor would be most unsuitable for the evening, and was now walking home in his own clothing through the pleasant evening air.

The soldier was thinking about the party that had just broken up. He pitied Agathos who was not able to forget the king even for one moment. As these thoughts ran through his mind, he heard a rustling in the trees by the side of the path. As quick as lightning the terrible form of the dragon stood before him.

Terror stricken, the soldier felt for the sharp sword the king had given him – but of course it was no longer at his side. There was nothing to help him now. As the soldier turned to run he realized the dragon had covered the ground with sharp darts – and he had left the king's sandals in the camp. The soldier fell to the ground, and the beast leapt on top of him.

Later that night two of his closest friends set out to look for him in the darkness. They neither wore their armor nor remembered the words of the king, for they knew nothing of the danger that was at hand. They, too, did not return to the camp, but the other soldiers continued to feast and enjoy themselves, and did not miss them until the morning.

The dragon was now gaining courage. It was afraid of the king, but these soldiers were not as dangerous as it had imagined they would be. It even thought of attacking the camp straight away, and destroying all the soldiers at once.

Then to the dragon's dismay Agathos took his turn at keeping guard. The dragon retreated to the wood that bordered the camp, uncertain what to do. It could see the sharp sword hanging by the side of Agathos, and the huge shield with the bright red cross on it, hung over his shoulder. It remembered his battle with the prince, and began to tremble as it decided to stay hidden.

The next morning Agathos had finished his turn of duty

and was sleeping in his tent. Other soldiers were on guard, but the dragon had no fear of them. With a mighty roar it rushed from the cover of the wood and attacked them tooth and nail. It tore at some with its cruel claws, it bit others with its sharp teeth, while still others it stung with lashes from its poisonous tail.

One soldier managed to reach his sword and lunged at the dragon, but because he had no helmet the dragon let its heavy claws crash down on the man's head.

Another soldier had found his sword and his helmet by this time. He was able to fight longer than the first, and wounded the dragon in its side. The outraged creature swung its tail at the soldier, and because the man was wearing no armor the sting penetrated and poisoned his body, leaving him seriously wounded.

Another man rushed from his tent. He seemed to be well armed, but in his hurry he had forgotten to pick up his shield. This soldier began to attack the dragon bravely. He wounded the creature in its neck and in one of its legs. Try as it could, the dragon could not get a hold on the man. Its claws kept slipping off soldier's helmet, and its sting was useless against the armor.

Suddenly, just as the soldier was pausing to rest, the enemy hurled a cluster of fiery darts. The sword was no defense against these, but the shield, left behind in his tent, would have protected him. Nursing his wounds the soldier staggered back to the camp, to fight no more.

The next soldier to attack was well prepared with his shield. But because the day was hot, he had not properly fastened the armor on his body. The dragon swept the soldier's shield and breastplate aside with its powerful claws, and this man too fell as the darts struck home. Other soldiers, without sandals on their feet, fell injured as they trod on the fiery darts that were strewn across the ground.

Some soldiers refused to come out of their tents, shaking with fear when they saw the wounds their companions had suffered. By now the enemy was attacking with increasing strength. Soon, it thought to itself, it would be able to get right into the camp and make the king's entire army helpless.

Agathos, meanwhile, was sleeping soundly in his tent after being on duty all night. In a dream he saw the prince standing before him, his hands and feet deeply wounded with the marks of nails. Underneath the prince lay the terrible enemy. Both had been severely injured in the fight, but the prince was victorious.

Agathos woke suddenly to hear the cries of his comrades and the terrifying roar of the dragon as it hurled itself into the camp. Agathos had always expected such an attack, which is why he wore his sandals at all times, and laid his armor beside his bed. He sprung to the ground and put it on. Then he fixed his sharp sword to his side and put his arm through the handle of his shield. Agathos was ready for battle.

At the door of his tent Agathos called on the king for strength, and then rushed forward. When the dragon saw him coming, it left off fighting the other soldiers and moved over to slay this soldier wearing the king's armor.

Agathos used his shield to protect himself from the fiery darts. Although he was beaten to his knees more than once, new strength came to him, and he quickly regained his feet and fought bravely against the merciless foe.

The battle was still raging as the sun went down. The good soldier was well nigh exhausted when he gathered his strength for one mighty blow. Calling aloud on the name of the prince, Agathos attacked the creature of evil so fiercely that it fled away.

As Agathos knelt to give thanks and praise, over the battlefield he could see the prince coming to him among the evening dew. He heard the prince's voice and saw his face.

"Well done, good and faithful servant," the prince said. "Come with me to my father's home."

When Agathos looked at the wounds in the hands and feet of the prince, he knew his dream had indeed been true.

"You are weary," the prince continued. "My father has a garden with a river as clear as crystal. Trees grow beside it, and their leaves will heal and revive you. Come to the home I have prepared for you."

Then Agathos was glad he had remained faithful to the king. Already the heat of the day and the fight with the evil enemy seemed like a fading dream. Soon he would meet with the loving king.

Epilogue on page 129

COBWEBS
Margaret Gatty

Twinette the spider was young and she was hungry. "It is time for you to weave yourself a web, my dear," her mother said one day. "Then you can catch flies for yourself. Only do not weave near me, for I am old and I like to stay in the corners where you will be in my way. Scramble away to a little distance off, and there you can spin. But make sure there is nothing below you before you begin. You will not catch anything to eat unless there is empty space for the flies to fly about in."

Twinette scrambled along a beam inside the church roof – for it was there that she lived with her mother – until she had gone what she thought might be a suitable distance. Then she stopped to look round. Considering she had eight eyes to look with, this was not difficult. But she was not so sure what might be below.

"I wonder if Mother would say there is nothing below me but empty space for flies about to fly in?" said she to herself.

So she went back to her mother and asked her what she thought.

"Oh dear, oh dear!" her mother said. "How can I think about what I don't see? There was nothing there in my younger days, I am sure, but everybody must find out for themselves. Let yourself down by your web and *see* if there is anything there or not."

Twinette thanked her mother for this advice, and was just moving away when another thought struck her. "How shall I *know* if there's anything there?" she asked.

"Dear me, if there is anything there, how can you help but *see* it?" her mother cried, irritated by her daughter's inquiring spirit. "You, with all those eyes in your head!"

"Thank you. Now I understand," Twinette said. Then scuttling back to the end of the beam she began to prepare her long line of web.

It was the most exquisite thing in the world – so fine you could scarcely see it; so elastic it could be blown about without breaking; such a perfect gray that it looked white against black things, and black against white; so manageable that Twinette could both make it with her spinnerets and travel down it all at once. And when she wished to get back, she could climb it and roll it up at the same time.

It was a wonderful silk line for anybody to make. But Twinette was not conceited. Line-making came naturally to her. She was about halfway down to the stone-flagged floor when she stopped to rest.

Balancing herself at the end of her line, with her legs crumpled up round her, she spoke to herself. "This is charming. It's all so nice here in the middle. Nice empty space for the flies to fly about in, and a very pleasant time they must have of it. Dear me, how hungry I feel. I must go back and weave my web at once."

Just as Twinette was preparing to roll up her silk line and be off, a ray of sunshine streamed through one of the windows and lit her suspended body – startling her with its dazzling brightness. Everything seemed in a blaze around her, and she turned round and round in terror.

"Oh dear, oh dear, oh dear!" she cried, for she did not know what else to say. Then, making a great effort, she gave one hearty spring, and blinded though she was, shot up to the roof as fast as a spider could go, rolling her silk line into a ball as she went. Once safely up, she stopped to grumble.

But it was dull work grumbling to herself, so she ran back to her mother in the corner.

"Back again so soon, my dear?" the old lady asked, not over-pleased at the fresh disturbance.

"That I'm back at all is a wonder," Twinette whimpered. "There's something down there, after all!"

"Why, what did you see?" her mother asked.

"Nothing. That was just it," Twinette answered. "I could see nothing for dazzle and blaze."

"Young people today are very troublesome with their observations," her mother remarked. "However, did this dazzle and blaze push you out of your place, my dear?"

Twinette said, "Certainly not. I came away by myself."

"Then how could they be anything?" her mother asked. "Two things cannot be in the same place at the same time."

Twinette sat very silent, wondering what dazzle and blaze could be if they were nothing at all. This was a question that might have puzzled her forever. Fortunately her mother interrupted by advising her to go and make a large web, for she really could not afford to feed Twinette out of her own web any longer.

"If dazzle and blaze kill me, you'll be sorry, Mother," Twinette complained.

"Nonsense about dazzle and blaze," the old spider cried, now thoroughly roused. "All you saw was bright light."

So Twinette scuttled off in silence. She dared not ask what bright light was made from, though she wanted very much to know.

But she felt too cross to begin to spin a large web. Even though she was hungry she preferred to search after truth rather than catch dinner, which showed she was no ordinary spider. So she resolved to go down below again and see if she could find a truly empty space.

She lowered herself a little further, and a very satisfactory journey she seemed to make.

"All is well so far," she said to herself, her good humor returning. "I do believe I've found nothing at last. How fine it is."

As she spoke, she hung dangling at the end of her long silk line, her legs tucked up round her as before, in perfect enjoyment. Suddenly the door of the church was thrown open. It was a windy evening, and the draught that poured in blew the silk line, with Twinette at the end of it, backwards and forwards through the air until she felt quite dizzy.

"Oh dear, oh dear," she cried. "What shall I do? How could anyone say there's nothing here, oh dear, but empty space for flies to fly about in?"

At last with much self-control she succeeded in coiling up her line, and hauled herself back to the church roof. She decided that her mother had no idea what she was talking about when she spoke of empty space with nothing in it.

Twinette scrambled along to her mother and told her what she thought, though not in plain words.

"If dazzle and blaze are nothing," Twinette cried at last, "how were we together in the same place? And down there I have found something else that is nothing, though it blows me out of my place twenty times in a minute. What is the use of believing things you cannot rely on, Mother? I don't think you know a quarter of what is down below!"

The old spider's head turned giddy with Twinette's line of reasoning, just as Twinette's head had done while she was swinging in the wind. "I cannot see it matters *what* is down there," she grumbled, "as long as there is room for flies to fly about in. I wish you would go back and spin."

But Twinette dawdled and thought, and thought and dawdled, until the day was nearly over.

"I will go down just once more," said she to herself at last, "and look around again."

And so she did, but this time she went even further. Halfway down she stopped to rest as usual. Presently, as she hung dangling in the air by her line, she grew braver. "I will find the end of it all," she thought. "I will see how far empty space goes." So saying, she continued spinning her long line of silk.

It was a wonderful line, certainly, or it would not have gone on to such a length without breaking. In a few minutes Twinette was on the floor. But she disliked the feel of the cold stone under her eight feet and began to run as fast as she could. Luckily she met with a step of woodwork on one side.

She hurried up the step and crept into a corner close by, where she stopped to take a breath. "One doesn't know what to expect in such strange places," she observed. "When I have rested I will go back, but I must wait until I can see a little better."

But seeing a little better was out of the question, for night was coming. So when she became weary of waiting,

Twinette stepped out of her hiding place to look round. The whole church was in darkness!

Now it is one thing for a spider to be snug in bed when it is dark, and quite another to be a long way from home and have lost your way. Twinette had often been in the dark corner with her mother, and thought nothing of it. But now she shook all over with fright, and wondered what sort of dreadful thing darkness could be. Then she thought of her mother's ideas of these things being nothing, and it made her angry.

"I cannot *see* anything, and I cannot *touch* anything," she murmured. "And yet there is *something* here, and it frightens me out of my wits."

At last her anxiety made her bold. She felt about for her line. It was there safe and sound, and she made a spring for it. Roll went the line, and up went Twinette; higher, higher, higher through the dark night air – seeing nothing, hearing nothing, feeling nothing but the desperate fear within. By the time she reached the roof she was exhausted and quickly fell asleep.

It must have been late next morning when she woke to the sound of organ music pealing through the church. The air vibrations swept pleasantly over her body, the music swelling and sinking like waves of the sea.

Twinette went down on her silk line to observe, but could see nothing that would account for her sensations. Fresh feelings, however, stole round her as she hung suspended, for it was a harvest festival and large white lilies were grouped with evergreens round the pillars. They filled the air with their powerful perfume, yet nothing disturbed Twinette from her place. Sunshine streamed in through the windows – she even felt it warm on her body – but it interfered with nothing else.

Meanwhile, in such a way as spiders hear, Twinette became aware of singing and prayer. A door opened and a breeze caught her line. But she held fast. So music and prayer and sunshine and breeze and scent were all there together. And Twinette was among them, and saw flies flying all around her.

This was enough. She went back to the roof, chose a home and began to spin. Before evening she had completed enough of her web to catch her first fly, which she feasted on. Then she cleared the remains away and sat down to think.

As she crossed and twisted and wove new threads to increase the size of her web, her ideas grew clearer and clearer. Each line she fastened brought its own understanding.

Cobwebs

"Two or three things *can* be in the same place at the same time." This part of the web seemed a little loose until she tightened it by a second line. "Sound and sunshine and wind don't drive each other out of their places." That held firm. "When one has feelings there must be something to cause them, whether one sees it or not." This was a wonderful thread. It went right round the web and was fastened down in several places.

"Light and darkness and sunshine and wind and sound and feelings and fright and pleasure don't keep away flies." She paused for breath. The interlacing threads looked strong as she placed them so carefully. "There must be so many things here that I don't know much about." The web got larger by the minute. "And there may be so many things beyond – ever so many things."

Twinette kept repeating these words until she finished her web. When she sat down after supper to think, she began to repeat them again – for she could think of nothing better or wiser to say. But this was no wonder, for all her thoughts put together made nothing but a cobweb, after all.

And when one day the broom swept the web with others from the church roof, Twinette was no longer there. She had died and handed down her cobweb-wisdom to another generation. But it was only cobweb-wisdom after all, for spiders remain spiders still. They weave their webs in the roofs of churches without understanding the mystery of unseen things on Earth – and the unseen mysteries of Heaven that even people cannot understand.

Epilogue on page 131

THE SPRING MORNING
Based on a story by Samuel Wilberforce

It was a spring beautiful morning in the large gardens surrounding a fine house. I watched four young people laughing as they walked through the long grass. At last they paused to rest by a gentle river that ran along the bottom of the garden, and refreshed themselves with wild strawberries that grew on its banks.
Suddenly they looked up from their eating as a man came through the trees bordering the garden.

"Look, it's the prince!" they called out together.

The man sat down in the shade and called the four around him. They appeared to know him, for they did not approach him as they would approach a stranger.

"Edward, Oliver, Rachel and Charlotte, I know you are

enjoying yourselves here," the man said quietly; "but you cannot stay much longer."

"But it's so good," the boy called Edward said. "I don't want to leave."

The prince shook his head. "It may look good to you, Edward, but believe me, by evening this garden will not be safe. The flowers will fade and the birds will sing no more. The water in the river will lose its freshness, and as the night grows darker you will see fierce eyes glaring out of the bushes."

"We can always go into the house," Edward said.

The prince shook his head. "There will be danger everywhere when night comes."

The four looked around in disbelief. Surely this could not be true, they whispered to each other.

The prince saw their faces and pointed into the distance. "Your real home is in that direction, with my father the king. Trust me, if you go there, you will be safe for ever."

"Is it easy to find this new home?" Edward asked.

"It is easy to know the way, but not always easy to get there," the prince replied. "To reach it you have to pass over steep hills and walk through dark places. Why, Rachel, you look puzzled."

"I'm wondering how we'll know when we've found the right place," she said. "There must be all sorts of houses out there."

"There are, but none of them is as good as the home I have prepared for you with my father. Your journey will be over when you come to a large palace surrounded by beautiful gardens. When you arrive, my father will be there to welcome you."

"Suppose we go the wrong way?" Rachel said anxiously. She sounded as though she always looked for difficulties. "Will we get lost for ever if we take a wrong turning?"

The prince smiled reassuringly. "You need have no fear, Rachel – as long as you follow my instructions carefully. I have already made the journey myself, and you will see my footprints along the path. But more than this, I shall walk with each of you, although you will not see me."

The boy named Edward spoke again. He looked to be the oldest. "Can the new home be better than this?"

'It is better than you can possibly imagine," the prince told him. "No danger can reach you there. There will be no darkness, no evil beasts to frighten or harm you. It is a home of love and peace and beauty."

Edward said it sounded so good that he wanted to set out as soon as possible. Charlotte and Oliver did not appear quite so certain, and Rachel wanted to know just how dangerous the journey would be.

"To a few travelers the way is safe and easy," the prince explained. "But many find it hard at times. Some hills are dangerous to climb, although others will be gentle on your feet. You must keep to the path I have made for you, but always remember I will help you every step of the way, if you ask. Come, Charlotte and Oliver, will you start on the journey first?"

"I'd rather stay here and enjoy myself until the afternoon," Oliver said awkwardly. "Will the journey be easier if we start now?"

The prince said that many found it to be so. "The path is surest and safest in the morning."

Charlotte picked another wild strawberry. "I'll stay with Oliver," she said. "It's a beautiful spring morning, and this garden is too beautiful to think of leaving yet. But I'll start soon. That's a promise."

"I cannot make you go," the prince replied. "But, see, I have a reed flute for each of you. When you play a few notes on it, you will know for certain that I am with you. The wild beasts along the way will flee when they hear it. If you are lost, or cannot pick out the path clearly, the music will make my footprints easier to follow."

All four took their flutes and blew on them. The music filled the garden with a beautiful harmony.

Edward and Rachel were already on their feet, ready to start their journey. Charlotte and Oliver remained on the ground. As the prince faded from their sight an argument broke out as to whether anyone had ever come to the garden at all.

Then Edward blew gently on his reed flute, and Rachel looked at him and smiled. She clapped her hands together and said there was not a moment to lose in setting out for the new home where the king's son was leading them.

"We'll catch up with you," Charlotte told Edward and Rachel. "You'll soon get tired, starting out so quickly. We may even reach the new home before you!" Then she laughed, and Oliver laughed with her.

"Not so," Edward replied. "The prince said the journey will be easier if we start out now. There's a much better place waiting for us, so why do you want to stay here a moment longer?"

Rachel bid her friends goodbye, urging them to start as soon as possible. But Charlotte and Oliver jeered, and picked up stones to throw at the two who had been their friends before the prince came to the garden.

"Be quick, Rachel," Edward urged. "The sun is already climbing above the hills." He could see that his friend looked frightened. "Listen," he said, "I'll blow on my reed flute."

He blew softly as they hurried away, and soon they were out of reach of the stones, and could hear the taunting voices no more.

So they walked on together, talking about the king's palace and some of the things they might find along the way.

"I wonder how long the journey will be," Edward said. "I'm longing to get safely to the end."

"I can't think about the end" Rachel replied. "We've only just set out, and to tell you the truth I'm scared of what lies ahead."

"Well, whatever there is, the king's palace must be wonderful if it's better than the garden we've just left," Edward said.

"And the king will be there," Rachel added thoughtfully, and that seemed to cheer her up. "But do you really believe his son is with us now?"

Edward said he really believed that he was. As they talked, they realized that the gentle path they had been walking along was becoming dry and stony. A stile across the way led into a barren valley.

Rachel held back. "I can see thorns," she said fearfully.

Edward paused. "But there's a path through them."

"If it's all the same to you," Rachel said, shivering, "I think I'll wait here."

"It's foolish to stop now," Edward protested. "Not only is Prince with us, but look, I can see his footprints on the path." And once again he played a few notes on his reed flute.

But Rachel refused to listen, either to Edward or to the music.

Edward jumped over the stile and began walking.

"Wait for me!" Rachel shouted in panic, getting to her feet.

The Spring Morning

"Then come quickly," Edward called back, for he was already some way along the stony path.

"Wait for just a moment," Rachel called. "I want to pick some fruit. We may not be able to find any along the path. It looks as though it leads through such a bleak valley."

"You mustn't delay," Edward urged. "The king's son will have food for us when we need it. If you stop to pick it now, you will slow us both down."

"Then I'll only pick a little," Rachel said, but she stayed a long time before crossing the stile.

"You're going much too fast," she complained to Edward  once she had caught up with him. "I'm waiting for Charlotte and Oliver. Perhaps they'll not be as keen to press on as you are."

Once more Edward begged Rachel to stay with him, and for a moment he almost succeeded. But try as he most certainly did, she could not be persuaded to continue the journey.

"There'll be time enough," she insisted. "Besides, the other two probably haven't even started out yet. See, I've done better than them by going early with you. If I wait here, you will be able to walk as fast as you like."

Edward, unable to convince his friend how important it was to keep on with the journey, was soon out of sight down the valley.

It was not long before Rachel began to feel frightened and alone. So she made her way back to the garden to find Charlotte and Oliver still resting by the bank of the river.

"You're back soon!" Oliver called.

Then he and Charlotte began to laugh as they thought of the hurry Rachel had been in to set off. But eventually Charlotte said that she wished she had set out with Edward, for she felt less inclined to go now than she had when the king's son had spoken to them.

As the sun rose higher in the sky, the three became good friends again and thought no more of Edward on his journey to the new home. By the middle of the day, when the sun was at its highest, the garden became too hot to do anything except lie down under a tree with their feet in the cool water of the river.

Charlotte said she kept thinking about Edward on his journey, and wondered if the sun was as hot for him. "Perhaps we should be leaving now," she told Oliver.

Oliver laughed. "What sort of person sets out on a journey when the sun is so high?" he sneered. "No, there will be time enough for us to start when it's cooler."

Charlotte sounded cross. "I wish I'd never stayed here with you. I should have set out with Edward and Rachel. Why, where's Rachel gone?"

While the two of them were arguing, Rachel had

The Spring Morning

glimpsed the king's son standing at the edge of the garden. She looked down at her reed flute and felt a strong desire to play on it. The sound of the music did not fill the garden, but the prince heard it, and once again he told Rachel of the home he had prepared for her. Gladly Rachel went out again on her journey, leaving her two quarreling friends behind.

Soon she came to the stile where she had left Edward earlier. The path through the valley now looked more thorny and dangerous, and the footprints Edward had followed were not so clear. The sun felt hot, and there was not a breath of wind. Nor was there any shelter. Edward would be far ahead. She sat on the stile and began to cry.

Edward was indeed far ahead. At first, after leaving Rachel, he felt sad and lonely. Then, as he played softly on his reed flute the certain feeling came over him that the king's son was with him, just as he had promised in the garden. Then Edward thought of the king who would be waiting to welcome him to his new home.

Soon his path became flat and easier. Before long he came to a river, and could see that at times it must flood after heavy rain, for sticks and dead leaves were caught in the branches of the trees that grew on the banks. The path continued on the far side, but the water was low and Edward found he could cross on the large rocks in the bed of the river.

As he left the river behind, the sun seemed to grow hotter and hotter, and suddenly Edward felt too tired to continue. Again he pulled his reed flute from his pocket and played a gentle tune. The path led past a dense flowering shrub. It looked as though it would make an excellent place to shelter until the sun was lower in the sky.

As Edward moved towards the bush, dark and coolly inviting inside, he was aware of someone holding him gently but firmly by the shoulder. He pulled away almost angrily, and would have sat down in the cool shade – when he saw a large snake watching him from the undergrowth.

Edward drew away in alarm. "Perhaps if I'd fallen asleep in there I would never have woken up," he exclaimed to himself. "That must have been the prince who held me back. I must press on with my journey. I can rest when I reach the king's palace."

As the sun scorched him, Edward played on the flute as he walked along. Immediately he felt refreshed and strengthened. Then as he looked ahead he realized that the path ran between some tall, shady trees. He hurried towards them, feeling the cool breeze blowing between the sturdy branches. Now he could make his way along the path quickly

The Spring Morning

and easily.

A little further on the trees grew more thickly, forming a dark wood. All around him, among the trees, he could see traps and snares.

"This will be a dangerous place at the end of the day," he said to himself. A sudden noise among the trees caused him to stop in fright. A great lion leapt out and crouched ready to spring – its long teeth flashing in the sunlight flickering through the trees.

Edward already had the reed flute in his hand. Loudly and urgently he played on it as his legs shook in terror. But at the first note the lion turned, and crept back between the trees, and Edward saw him no more. Instead of the angry growl, there came a voice with a refreshing breeze. "Blow on your flute at all times," the voice said.

"The prince," Edward thought to himself as he recognized the voice.

As Edward passed out of the wood, before him in the far distance he saw a beautiful building surrounded by large gardens. At the edge of the gardens was a high wall with a door set in it, golden and shining. This must be the palace where the king lived. It would be the end of his journey.

He wanted to run, but his feet were aching and he knew there was still some way to go. Now that he was out in the open, the sun beat down on his head again and seemed even hotter than before.

He wondered whether to return to the shelter of the wood, but as he played on his reed flute the way ahead became easier and the sun became less hot. By the side of the road he found a shelter built from leafy branches, with a notice from the king saying travelers were allowed to rest there awhile.

Being footsore and weary, Edward needed no further invitation. As he sat down, he began to play softly on his reed flute. As he played, the sky clouded over and a terrifying storm swept across the land. The rain fell in torrents, and he could hear the wild beasts roaring in the wood. But in his shelter Edward felt no fear, for the prince who had invited him to make the journey was there with him, unseen.

At last the sky began to clear, and Edward set out to continue on his way. The sun was now past its hottest place in the sky, and a cool breeze blew on his face. He moved speedily on, and thought perhaps it would not be long before he reached the golden door that would take him into the palace gardens and his new home.

Rachel was a long way behind. She had stayed at the stile

unable to bring herself to follow Edward – until she realized how much time she had wasted already. Soon it might be too late to start. So, gathering up all her courage, Rachel climbed quickly over the stile onto the stony path.

Was it her imagination, or was the path narrower than it had been earlier? It was certainly hard-going now. The thorns tore at her feet and ankles, and for a moment she felt inclined to return to the garden. Then she remembered the reed flute that had been such a help to Edward. At first Rachel was unable to play any sort of tune, but the long, sad note that came from it was enough to let her know that the king's son was holding her hand and leading her carefully along the path where it was safest to walk.

"I really do want you with me," she whispered. "I will try harder to please you next time, because I want to reach the palace."

Then came a quiet but definite voice in the breeze. "You are not able to earn a place with me in the palace," the voice said. "You must accept it as a gift."

Rachel fell to the ground in dismay. "I can't. I want to *deserve* the reward at the end."

"That is not possible," the voice answered.

Rachel did not answer, but stood up and began to hurry over the open ground. "I *must* make sure the king lets me into the new home," she said to herself.

At that moment the storm, which had passed over the

shelter where Edward had been resting, beat down on Rachel. The rain fell in torrents, and fierce gusts of wind swept past, while the pealing thunderclouds seemed to come down all around.

The ground quickly turned to mud, making Rachel slip and fall as she tried to hurry forward. She saw a hill ahead, and struggled to the top, for surely to press on like this would be enough to please the king.

Once over the hill, which provided no break from the storm, Rachel came to the river that Edward had crossed so easily. Now it had swollen into a roaring torrent that dashed along, foaming and boiling, carrying all in its course.

What should she do? Either she must venture into the river to get to the far bank, or else give up all idea of reaching the new home that was waiting for her. She had already made up her mind not to ask for help.

The large rocks in the river were not fully covered by the raging water. So, plucking up a little courage, Rachel started to creep along by holding onto them. First the water was ankle deep, then knee deep, then it rushed past her waist. Still she kept on, clinging tightly to the rocks. One more step

The Spring Morning

and the water covered her shoulders, sweeping her feet off the ground.

In panic, Rachel managed to clutch onto a jagged rock before she could be carried away and drowned. She was not nearly through the river – what if the next step should carry her away altogether?

The reed flute was in her pocket, and she knew she could reach it if she tried. But Rachel thought only of getting to the far bank. Each rock proved harder to reach than the last, and the water seemed to grow colder by the minute.

She could stand the force of the river no longer. Then it seemed to her that she could make out the king's son standing beside her in the fast-running torrent.

"My flute! My reed flute!" something seemed to say inside her.

Caring nothing for her safety now, Rachel let go of the rock to which she had been clinging so desperately, and reached for her flute. Even before she played it, she felt herself being lifted from the raging waters and placed safely on the grassy bank on the far side of the angry river.

"I'm trying so hard to get to the palace," she said earnestly. "Please forgive me for getting it so wrong. I promise I'll do better from now on."

"Do you still not understand what I am telling you, Rachel? Your own strength will never be enough to get you safely to the end of your journey."

Rachel lay on the riverbank, exhausted. "If I'm so weak, how can I ever get there?"

"You *still* do not understand," the voice of the prince continued. "It is in your weakness that I want you to come to me. You are not able to earn my love. Will you trust me now?"

And there, on the safety of the river bank, Rachel wept. Now, at last, she could see that the king's son loved her – not because she deserved it, which she didn't, but simply because he wanted her to be with him in the safety of the new home.

Rachel rose slowly to her feet. "Forgive me," she said. "I will keep going if you come with me."

She could no longer see the prince, but Rachel knew he was there. It seemed to her that he was smiling and putting a caring arm around her shoulder.

"Have I not been with you always?" his voice seemed to say. "It was you who did not understand that I was with you."

At this very moment, Edward was on a hill overlooking the palace and its gardens. The setting sun hung low over the far hills and poured its golden brightness over everything. Rich and beautiful did the palace shine out before his joyful eyes. And as he looked, he thought he could make out people in the gardens, wearing robes of light and crowns that looked like living fire.

He ran down the hill and hurried to the golden door set in the high wall, his heart full of hope and joy. The troubles of the way were over. He looked back over his shoulder at the path he had trodden, and it seemed that all his difficulties had been no more than a preparation for this happy home.

He remembered the scorching sun no more. The weary pathway through the valley, the evil wood, the lion's fierce face, the storm: all these seemed as nothing compared to the splendid home that was awaiting him now. His only thought was to thank the king and his son who had brought him safely through. As he lifted up his eyes, he saw a sign over the door, which said, "Knock, the door will be opened."

Edward knocked with all his strength. The golden door swung wide and he entered the palace gardens.

Rachel, meanwhile, was entering the forest. As she came among the dark trees, the sun had already set. The branches shut out what little moonlight there was, making the path almost impossible to see. But Rachel feared nothing. She played constantly on her reed flute and gained strength and courage.

At times her feet tangled in traps set by the side of the path, but they did not hold her for long. Then Rachel heard the dreadful roaring from the lion that had terrified Edward.

Throwing her reed flute to the ground in panic, she ran for the safety of the open ground she could see dimly in front. But it seemed that the king's son was holding her back. Quickly she retrieved her flute and played on it once more. Then there was no need to run, for Rachel knew she was safe from all danger.

Once outside the wood, it was too dark to see the leafy shelter where Edward had rested during the storm. Indeed, there was no time to be lost in reaching her new home. Rachel pressed on wearily, sometimes remembering to play on her reed flute and be helped, and at other times trying to get through the difficulties in her own way. But always the king's son walked with her in the darkness.

At last she drew near the shining golden door in the high wall surrounding the palace gardens. The soft and gentle sounds of music from within gave her fresh hope. With a fast-beating heart she seized the golden knocker and – oh, joy of joys! – the door swung open into a beautiful garden where the sun shone day and night. Then poor, wavering Rachel entered the heavenly palace.

The Spring Morning

But what had Charlotte and Oliver been doing? Had they begun their journey? Perhaps they were soon to reach the golden door.

After Rachel had slipped away, to start once more on her journey, Charlotte and Oliver sat a while longer on the grassy bank beside the river.

There seemed to be so little to do, and anyway the sun was still high in the sky. Charlotte fell asleep in the shade while Oliver wandered away, searching for fresh fruit from the many trees and bushes.

The evening darkness came suddenly. Oliver had been sitting with the fruit he had picked, throwing stones into the river. The first sign of danger came without warning. The growl of some large and savage beast frightened him. He looked round for Charlotte and saw her still sleeping on the grassy bank.

The reed flute fell from Oliver's pocket, and he would have picked it up but the beast was coming closer. It seemed that the flute would be of little use now. Far better, he decided, to use his own fast legs and run from the garden. Was there not a path to the new home? If he tried, could he not get there in time? He was proud of the way he could deal with problems.

Charlotte woke suddenly. She had heard a cry. The garden was now silent. Oliver had gone. Darkness was all around her. As she stood up, she realized her flute had rolled down the hill while she was sleeping. It was now bent and damaged, and she doubted it would play music any more.

But as she retrieved it and placed it to her lips, blowing a long, sad note, the king's son appeared before her.

"You must take me from here," she begged in tears. "Only you can save me now. Take me to the new home you've prepared for me." She asked for forgiveness as Rachel had done, and this was freely given.

Then the prince lifted Charlotte onto his strong shoulders and carried her safely through the raging torrent and the dark wood. For her, too, the shining door swung open to let her into the heavenly home.

As Charlotte blinked in the bright sunlight, Edward and Rachel came forward to greet her, and exchange stories of their journeys. Charlotte began to cry.

"What's the matter?" Rachel asked. "This new home is the happiest place there could ever be."

"You deserve to be here," Charlotte told her. "I am only here because the king's son carried me."

Edward smiled. "There is not one person here who can boast that they deserve this beautiful home. Come on, let's go and meet the king. He will receive you, because his son brought you here in love. Without him, none of us could have made the journey."

As Edward spoke, a feeling of power and perfect peace

The Spring Morning

filled the palace gardens. The king appeared, smiling.

"Come," he said, as they looked up at him in wonder. "Come, Charlotte, I will dry your tears. Come, Edward; come, Rachel."

And the three stepped forward.

Epilogue on page 133

EPILOGUES

THE KING AND HIS SERVANTS

The Bible says we can never earn our way to Heaven by doing good things, but we all have different gifts and talents. If we belong to Jesus we have to serve him. Jesus told  several stories about people buying and selling, and made it clear that we must not waste our time here on earth. As this story shows, not everyone has the same talents. The tears were as valuable as the jewels. Don't forget, one day the trumpet will sound, and it will be too late to do all the things for the Lord God that we keep meaning to do.

Some Bible verses:
[Jesus said] "Be on the alert then, for you do not know the day nor the hour. For it is just like a man about to go on a journey, who called his own slaves and entrusted his possessions to them. To one he gave five talents, to another, two,

and to another, one, each according to his own ability; and he went on his journey. Immediately the one who had received the five talents went and traded with them, and gained five more talents. In the same manner the one who had received the two talents gained two more." (Matthew 25:13-17, but read up to verse 30 for the whole parable on which this story is loosely based, and see what happens to the servant who wasted his one talent.)

[Jesus] has said, "I will never desert you, nor will I ever forsake you," so that we confidently say, "The Lord is my helper, I will not be afraid. What will man do to me?" (Hebrews 13:5b-6)

A LESSON OF FAITH

Just because we cannot understand something, it doesn't mean it's not true. Some people say we can't be certain there's a place for us in Heaven. Jesus came from Heaven and made many promises, and then He went back there when He rose from the dead. So we really can trust Him when He says He will take us to Heaven to be with Him when we die – as long as we accept him as our Savior. When we do, Jesus promises to forgive all we have ever done wrong, and we can trust Him absolutely. There is one part of this story that is not like life for us. Did you notice it at the beginning? The Bible teaches that unlike the butterfly, we will remember our life here as "caterpillars"!

Some Bible verses:
For the word of the cross is foolishness to those who are perishing, but to us who are being saved it is the power of God. (1 Corinthians 1:18)

Therefore, having been justified by faith, we have peace with God through our Lord Jesus Christ. (Romans 5:1)

Epilogues

Now faith is the assurance of things hoped for, the conviction of things not seen. (Hebrews 11:1)

[Jesus says] "I give eternal life to them, and they will never perish; and no one will snatch them out of My hand." (John 10:28)

THE ROCKY ISLAND

The disciples of Jesus were caught out in the large lake of Galilee in a couple of violent storms. Like many of us when things in the Christian life get tough, they were afraid. But Jesus had words of peace and comfort for them. Here is one occasion when the disciples were scared.

Some Bible verses:
On that day, when evening came, He [Jesus] said to them, "Let us go over to the other side." Leaving the crowd, they took Him along with them in the boat, just as He was; and other boats were with Him.

And there arose a fierce gale of wind, and the waves were breaking over the boat so much that the boat was already filling up. Jesus Himself was in the stern, asleep on the cushion; and they woke Him and said to Him, "Teacher, do you not care that we are perishing?"

And He got up and rebuked the wind and said to the sea, "Hush, be still." And the wind died down and it became perfectly calm. And He said to them, "Why are you afraid? Do you still have no faith?"

Epilogues

They became very much afraid and said to one another, "Who then is this, that even the wind and the sea obey Him?" (Mark 4:35-41)

"Peace I leave with you; My peace I give to you; not as the world gives do I give to you. Do not let your heart be troubled, nor let it be fearful." (John 14:27)

WAITING

Why am I here? Have you ever asked God that question? Whether we have great abilities, or many disabilities, the Lord God has a purpose for each one of us. There is something that only *you* can do for Him. So let's stop complaining about life being unfair or boring. Find out how *you* can serve the Lord.

Some Bible verses:
[Jesus said,] "Then the King will say to those on His right, 'Come, you who are blessed of My Father, inherit the kingdom prepared for you from the foundation of the world. For I was hungry, and you gave Me something to eat; I was thirsty, and you gave Me something to drink; I was a stranger, and you invited Me in; naked, and you clothed Me; I was sick, and you visited Me; I was in prison, and you came to Me.'

"Then the righteous will answer Him, 'Lord, when did we see You hungry, and feed You, or thirsty, and give You something to drink? And when did we see You a stranger, and invite You in, or naked, and clothe You? When did we see You sick, or in prison, and come to You?'

Epilogues

"The King will answer and say to them, 'Truly I say to you, to the extent that you did it to one of these brothers of Mine, even the least of them, you did it to Me.' (Matthew 25:34-40, but read the rest of the chapter to find out what happens to those who lived their lives so selfishly that they never even noticed people who were in need.)

What use is it, my brethren, if someone says he has faith but he has no works? Can that faith save him? If a brother or sister is without clothing and in need of daily food, and one of you says to them, "Go in peace, be warmed and be filled," and yet you do not give them what is necessary for their body, what use is that? Even so faith, if it has no works, is dead, being by itself. (James 2:14-17)

Chris Wright

THE WANDERERS

The Bible tells us that the world is a fallen place where we are born without knowing the Lord God, rather like the land where Leo and Zimri first lived. Jesus rescues us and washes us clean, then welcomes us into God's family as His children.

Even when we belong to God's family we will often stray, so like Zimri we must be quick to call to Him for forgiveness. Then He will bring us to safety. It is right to pray for our own family and friends, and tell them about Jesus, but Jesus cannot make anyone come to Him if they do not want Him.

Some Bible verses:
[Jesus said] "What man among you, if he has a hundred sheep and has lost one of them, does not leave the ninety-nine in the open pasture and go after the one which is lost until he finds it? When he has found it, he lays it on his shoulders, rejoicing. And when he comes home, he calls together his friends and his neighbors, saying to them, 'Rejoice with me, for I have found my sheep which was lost!' I tell you that in the same way, there will be more joy in heaven over one sinner who repents than over ninety-nine righteous persons who need no repentance." (Luke 15:4-7)

Epilogues

If we confess our sins, He [Jesus] is faithful and righteous to forgive us our sins and to cleanse us from all unrighteousness. (1 John 1:9)

Now He [Jesus] was telling them a parable to show that at all times they ought to pray and not to lose heart. (Luke 18:1)

NOT LOST, BUT GONE BEFORE!

Like the nymph not trusting the frog, maybe we sometimes wonder if Heaven really exists. Has anyone ever returned from the dead to tell us about it? Yes, Jesus has. If we could see that new life now, think how excited we would be. But with our human bodies, how much would we understand – even if such a thing were possible? Even though we cannot understand everything, Jesus, the Son of God, has promised to take us to Heaven one day in perfect safety.

Some Bible verses:
[Saint Paul is writing this letter while many of the people who saw Jesus after His death are still alive.] For I delivered to you as of first importance what I also received, that Christ died for our sins according to the Scriptures, and that He was buried, and that He was raised on the third day according to the Scriptures, and that He appeared to Cephas [Peter], then to the twelve.

After that He appeared to more than five hundred brethren at one time, most of whom remain until now, but some have fallen asleep; then He appeared to James, then to all the apostles. (1 Corinthians 15:3-7)

Epilogues

[Jesus said] "Do not let your heart be troubled; believe in God, believe also in Me. In My Father's house are many dwelling places; if it were not so, I would have told you; for I go to prepare a place for you. If I go and prepare a place for you, I will come again and receive you to Myself, that where I am, there you may be also. (John 14:1-3)

In the hope of eternal life, which God, who cannot lie, promised long ages ago. (Titus 1:2)

AGATHOS

A scary story, and one that we must take as a great warning. Saint Peter in the New Testament writes that God's enemy, the devil, prowls around like a roaring lion, but we needn't be afraid if we keep close to Jesus. Saint Paul tells us about the armor we must wear if we are to live a strong Christian life. So let's be like Agathos, not like the careless soldiers who thought there was no need to bother.

Some Bible verses:
[Saint Paul wrote] Be strong in the Lord and in the strength of His might. Put on the full armor of God, so that you will be able to stand firm against the schemes of the devil. For our struggle is not against flesh and blood, but against the rulers, against the powers, against the world forces of this darkness, against the spiritual forces of wickedness in the heavenly places.

Therefore, take up the full armor of God, so that you will be able to resist in the evil day, and having done everything, to stand firm.

Stand firm therefore, having girded your loins with truth, and having put on the breastplate of righteousness, and having shod your feet with the preparation of the gospel of peace; in addition to all, taking up the shield of faith with which you will be able to extinguish all the flaming arrows of the evil one. And take the helmet of salvation, and the sword of the Spirit, which is the word of God.

With all prayer and petition pray at all times in the Spirit, and with this in view, be on the alert. (Ephesians 6:10-18)

COBWEBS

I used to think this story was about understanding the Trinity, the mystery of God the Father, God the Son, and God the Holy Spirit. But reading it now, I think Margaret Gatty was simply writing about how difficult it is to understand so many things, both on Earth and in Heaven. In that way we are all like Twinette. Yet the story does help us understand a little about the Trinity. Think of God as the church building, and in it are the glorious sounds of  the organ that fill the church (the Father), the dazzling light (Jesus, the Light of the World), and the wind (the Holy Spirit). So three things can be in the building, in the same place, at the same time – and be separate and yet one. It's not a perfect picture, but it may help.

Some Bible verses:
"Holy, Holy, Holy, is the LORD of hosts, the whole earth is full of His glory." (Isaiah 6:3)

Then Jesus again spoke to them, saying, "I am the Light of the world; he who follows Me will not walk in the darkness, but will have the Light of life." (John 6:12)

Epilogues

[Jesus said] "Do not be amazed that I said to you, 'You must be born again.' The wind blows where it wishes and you hear the sound of it, but do not know where it comes from and where it is going; so is everyone who is born of the Spirit." (John 3:7-8)

[Jesus said] "I and the Father are one." (John 10:30)

[Jesus said] "If anyone loves Me, he will keep My word; and My Father will love him, and We will come to him and make Our abode with him. (John 14:23)

The grace of the Lord Jesus Christ, and the love of God, and the fellowship of the Holy Spirit, be with you all. (2 Corinthians 13:14)

THE SPRING MORNING

It took a long time for Rachel to realize there was no way she could work their own way to the safety of the king's palace. She seemed to think that if only she tried harder, she would get there in the end. But as the king's son says in this story, his love and forgiveness are gifts Rachel could not earn. And Charlotte too could not get there in her own strength, nor could Edward. So, the real King's Son, Jesus, takes us to Heaven not because of how well we're doing in life, but because we tell Him we cannot possibly get there on our own. But we have to ask Him to take us there, something that Oliver failed to do. And this is His reply:

Some Bible verses:
[Jesus said] "For everyone who asks receives; he who seeks finds; and to him who knocks, the door will be opened." (Luke 11:10)

Epilogues

"The Lord is not slow about His promise, as some count slowness, but is patient toward you, not wishing for any to perish but for all to come to repentance. (2 Peter 3:9)

For by grace you have been saved through faith; and that not of yourselves, it is the gift of God; not as a result of works, so that no one may boast. (Ephesians 2:8-9)

Chris Wright

THE WRITERS

MARGARET GATTY

Margaret Gatty was born in England in 1809. Her father, the Reverend A. J. Scott, was chaplain to Admiral Nelson, and at the battle of Trafalgar it was claimed by the family at the time that Nelson died while Scott was holding him.

Margaret married the Reverend Alfred Gatty in Ecclesfield, Yorkshire in 1839, and they shared a great interest in natural history. Not only did Margaret edit and write stories for *Aunt Judy's Tales* for children, she wrote academic books on natural history that earned her much respect in the scientific world.

Children's stories based on natural history are probably Margaret Gatty's best known writings. Some were first published in 1855 as *Parables from Nature Series 1*, combining her love of science and nature with her love of God. Three other series of short stories followed, and later editions combined all four books.

Margaret Gatty gave birth to six sons and four daughters, although some died in infancy. Margaret died after a long illness in October 1873, although her husband lived until 1903. In St. Mary's Church in Ecclesfield there is a memorial window to Margaret, known as the Parable Window, paid for by more than one thousand children: *as a token of love and gratitude for the many books she wrote for them.*

SAMUEL WILBERFORCE

Samuel Wilberforce was born in England in 1805, and was ordained as a Church of England clergyman in 1828. He later became Bishop of Oxford and then Winchester. He was the son of William Wilberforce, the MP who is remembered today for leading the anti slave-trade movement.

In 1840 Samuel Wilberforce published a book called *Agathos and Other Sunday Stories*, and later a companion to it called *The Rocky Island and Other Similitudes*. The stories were later published in a single volume called *Agathos and The Rocky Island and Other Sunday Stories*. The allegories in this book come from this larger volume.

In the foreword of an early edition, Wilberforce writes: *The following allegories and stories have been actually related by the Author to his children on successive Sunday evenings.* The stories were so popular that by 1900 over fifty editions had been printed.

Samuel Wilberforce died in July 1873, near Leatherhead in Surrey, after a serious fall from his horse.

CHRIS WRIGHT

Chris Wright is the author of over thirty books, starting with young fiction for an English Christian publisher in 1966. He has written both fiction and non-fiction, mostly with a Christian theme, for a variety of publishers. Chris is married with three grownup children, and lives in the West Country of England where he is a home group leader with his local church. His personal website is: www.rocky-island.com

MARY JONES ADVENTURE BOOK
(ENDORSED BY BIBLE SOCIETY)
Chris Wright
ISBN: 978-1-935079-20-0
Lighthouse Christian Publishing

Take part in Mary Jones' adventure! Mary Jones saved for six years to buy a Bible of her own - and after walking 26 miles (over 40km) to get it, she discovered there were none for sale! Mary made her walk alone, barefoot over a mountain pass and through deep valleys in Wales in 1800, at the age of 15.

You can travel with her today in this book as you follow the clues and solve the puzzles. You, too, will get to Bala where Mary traveled, and if you're really quick you may be able to "buy" a Bible just like Mary's!

The true story of Mary Jones and her Bible has captured the imagination for more than 200 years. For this book, Chris Wright has delved deep into the records and come up with the latest facts that are known about Mary.

Packed with puzzles, photographs of real places, and all sorts of fascinating information. If a puzzle is too difficult, or you just don't like puzzles at all, you can turn the page and keep reading. Solving puzzles is part of the fun, but the story is still there to read and enjoy whether you have a go at the puzzles or not. Can you discover the real story of Mary Jones?

PILGRIM'S PROGRESS PUZZLE BOOK
Chris Wright
ISBN: 978-0-9797863-3-4
Lighthouse Christian Publishing

Travel with young Christian as he sets out on a difficult and perilous journey to find the King. Solve the puzzles and riddles along the way, to help Christian reach the Celestial City. Then travel with his friend Christiana. She has four young brothers who can sometimes be a bit of a problem.

Be warned, you will meet giants and lions - and even dragons! There are people who don't want Christian and Christiana to reach the safety of the King and his Son. But not everyone is an enemy. There are plenty of friendly people. It's just a matter of finding them.

Are you prepared to help? Are you sure? The journey can be very dangerous! By the way, you can enjoy the story even if you don't want to try the puzzles.

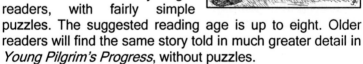

This is a book for younger readers, with fairly simple puzzles. The suggested reading age is up to eight. Older readers will find the same story told in much greater detail in *Young Pilgrim's Progress*, without puzzles.

YOUNG PILGRIM'S PROGRESS
Chris Wright
ISBN: 978-0-9797863-2-7
Lighthouse Christian Publishing

This book will be a great favorite with young readers, as well as with families, Sunday School teachers, and anyone who wants to read John Bunyan's *Pilgrim's Progress* in a clear form. All the old favorites are here: Christian, Christiana, the Wicket Gate, Interpreter, Hill Difficulty with the lions, the four sisters at the House Beautiful, Vanity Fair, Giant Despair, Faithful and Talkative – and, of course, Greatheart. The list is almost endless.

The first part of the story is told by Christian himself, as he leaves the City of Destruction to reach the Celestial City, and becomes trapped in the Slough of Despond near the Wicket Gate. On his journey he will encounter lions, giants, and a creature called the Destroyer.

Christiana follows along later, and tells her own story in the second part. Not only does Christiana have to cope with her four young brothers, she worries about whether her clothes are good enough for meeting the King. Will she find the dangers in Vanity Fair that Christian found? Will she be caught by Giant Despair and imprisoned in Doubting Castle? What about the dragon with seven heads?

It's a dangerous journey, but Christian and Christiana both know that the King's Son is with them, helping them through the most difficult parts until they reach the Land of Beulah, and see the Celestial City on the other side of the Dark River. This is a story you will remember forever, and it's about a journey you can make for yourself.

ZEPHAN AND THE VISION
Chris Wright
ISBN: 978-0-9773766-1-2
Lighthouse Christian Publishing

An exciting story of the adventures of two angels who seem to know almost nothing - until they have a vision!

Two ordinary angels are caring for the distant Planet Eltor, and they are about to get a big shock - they are due to take a trip to the Planet Earth! This is Zephan's story of the vision he is given before being allowed to travel with Talora, his companion angel, to help two young people fight against the enemy.

There's a difficulty. Everybody on Earth looks like a small castle. Some castles are strong and built in good positions, while others appear weak and open to attack. But it seems that the best-looking castles are not always the most secure.

Meet Castle Nadia and Castle Max, the two castles that Zephan and Talora have to defend. And meet the nasty creatures who have built shelters for themselves around the back of these castles. And worst of all, meet the shadow angels who live in a cave on Shadow Hill. This is a story about the forces of good and the forces of evil. Who will win the battle for Castle Nadia?

The events in this story are based very loosely on John Bunyan's allegory, The Holy War.

Made in the USA